Relational Inclusivi..., ...
the Elementary Classroom

Learn how to support and encourage the development of strong, nurturing relationships among your students of all neurotypes and needs with this practical, field-tested guide. Featuring classroom lessons, group activities, and a toolkit for creating social network maps specific to your classroom, this book shows teachers how to easily implement inclusive practices into their daily school routines. The book is anchored within a Research Practice Partnership that demonstrates how teachers can use simple research tools to gather real-time information about student relationships in their classrooms. Teachers can use this data to organize student groupings and plan classroom activities that support relational inclusivity. Moving beyond transactional approaches, like behavioral regulation and rule setting, this book prioritizes relationship building as vital to fostering inclusive classroom communities. It is key reading for in-service educators striving to create the kind of learning environment that meets the socio-emotional needs of all learners. Pre-service educators, educational researchers, and administrators can also use this helpful resource to support ongoing professional development that prioritizes a student's sense of belonging and social emotional development in school.

Dr. Christoforos Mamas is a former elementary school teacher and is currently an associate professor specializing in Transforming Special Education within the Department of Education Studies at the University of California, San Diego. His main research focus revolves around investigating the relational inclusivity of students identified as having special educational needs and disabilities in mainstream educational environments.

Dr. Shana R. Cohen is a former early childhood educator and is currently an associate professor in the Education Studies

Department at the University of California, San Diego. Her research examines immigrant families' socialization processes in rearing their neurodiverse children. Her current work uses community engaged partnerships to develop sustainable pedagogical tools and interventions for multilingual and neurodiverse learners.

Caren Holtzman is a former classroom teacher and retired faculty member in the Education Studies Department at the University of California. Her current work focuses on innovative programs that support the academic and social-emotional growth of traditionally marginalized students including newcomers and housing-insecure youth.

Relational Inclusivity in the Elementary Classroom

A Teacher's Guide to Supporting Student Friendships and Building Nurturing Communities

Christoforos Mamas, Shana R. Cohen, and Caren Holtzman

Routledge
Taylor & Francis Group

NEW YORK AND LONDON

Designed cover image: Getty images

First published 2024
by Routledge
605 Third Avenue, New York, NY 10158

and by Routledge
4 Park Square, Milton Park, Abingdon, Oxon, OX14 4RN

Routledge is an imprint of the Taylor & Francis Group, an informa business

© 2024 Christoforos Mamas, Shana Cohen, and Caren Holtzman

The right of Christoforos Mamas, Shana Cohen, and Caren Holtzman
to be identified as authors of this work has been asserted in accordance
with sections 77 and 78 of the Copyright, Designs and Patents Act 1988.

ISBN: 978-1-032-50488-9 (hbk)
ISBN: 978-1-032-49818-8 (pbk)
ISBN: 978-1-003-29873-8 (ebk)

DOI: 10.4324/9781003398738

Typeset in Palatino
by KnowledgeWorks Global Ltd.

Acknowledgements

This journey has been an intricate mosaic crafted from the pieces of dedication, collaboration, and unwavering support from a multitude of individuals who have played pivotal roles in the success of our research-practice partnership. As we express our gratitude, we acknowledge that their contributions are immeasurable, and their impact enduring.

We extend our deepest appreciation to our colleague, Rusty Bresser, who read drafts of the book and gave us invaluable feedback to make the chapters meaningful to educators. We would also like to acknowledge all the teachers by name (please see list below) who stood at the forefront of our initiative. Your commitment to fostering relational inclusivity in your classrooms has been the driving force behind our endeavors. Your enthusiasm, openness, and tireless efforts have not only shaped the course of our research-practice partnership but also have shown us your commitment to supporting your students' social-emotional development. We appreciate your generous gifts of time, open doors, willingness to try out early iterations of the Social Network Analysis (SNA) Toolkit, and creative and thoughtful ideas for classroom activities that continually inspire students to build deep connections with you and with each other. Thank you!

Malini Asher
Makenzie Brito
Bailey Choi
Christian Demesa
Thy Dinh
Kristy Drake
Erin Epstein
Kim Guzman
Leah Hodgins
Cathy Huynh

Maureen Jackson
Nilu Karunasiri
Ali Kayatta
Judy Kozak
Adele Lawrence
Rachel Lopez
Dan Ly
Natalie Matsuura
Kathrina Mendez
Madison Murrillo

Susan Robbins
Mary Scott
Kathy Seckington
Jami Smith
Nikki Szudlo
Curtis Taylor
Erika Tinoco
Jamison Treger
Adrienne Villarreal

A very special appreciation and acknowledgment goes to the students who embraced the spirit of relational inclusivity with open hearts and minds. Your willingness to engage in the process, share your experiences, and actively participate in our initiatives has been inspiring. You are the reason we strive for meaningful change, and your perspectives have enriched our understanding immeasurably. We are indebted not only to the elementary students who participated in our project, but also to our UCSD Education Studies students who asked wonderful questions, contributed thoughtful insights, and considered how a focus on relational inclusivity might impact their future work in classrooms.

To the dedicated paraprofessionals, such as Paul Shutz, Paul Holtzman, and Sarah Lewis who worked alongside the teachers supporting students, we extend our heartfelt thanks. Your attention to detail, organizational prowess, and unwavering support have been the bedrock upon which our partnership has flourished. Your commitment to creating an environment conducive to growth and learning has been instrumental in bringing our vision to life.

We express our gratitude to the administrators and principals who recognized the importance of this work and provided the necessary teacher encouragement, planning time, and resources for their staff. Your belief in the transformative power of relational inclusivity has been instrumental in amplifying our impact and reaching new heights. A special thank you to Dr. Kathleen Gallagher and Dr. Melissa Han for opening their schools to our work and giving their teachers time to engage in learning with us.

Finally, to our families and friends who stood by us with unwavering support, understanding, and encouragement throughout this journey, we extend our deepest gratitude. Your patience and belief in our mission have been the pillars that sustain us through the challenges and triumphs.

In acknowledging each individual who contributed to this book, we recognize that it is the collective effort of a diverse and dedicated community that has propelled us forward. This work stands as a testament to what can be achieved when hearts and minds come together in pursuit of a common goal—promoting relational inclusivity in elementary education.

Contents

Figures and Tables

Figures

Tables

Overview

This book was designed to elevate Social Emotional Learning (SEL) in the classroom and integrate SEL across the content areas and throughout the day. Our motivation for writing this book stems from our work with classroom teachers and our growing understanding of the importance of the relationships between students in the classroom. Teachers who prioritize *Relational Inclusivity* (RI), which is based on a social network perspective, gauge the meaningful engagement of all students across key social aspects of schooling. Our previous research identified four primary networks that encompass the majority of students' social interactions at school: friendship, recess/play, academic support, and emotional well-being networks. Teachers who pay attention to these social aspects will have students who feel like they belong in their classrooms, and who are motivated to learn.

This book provides a set of tools for teachers to measure and nurture RI in their classrooms. The Social Network Analysis (SNA) Toolkit we describe in this book is designed to understand how children are connected to each other in their classrooms during structured learning times and during unstructured outside play time. Teachers can use findings from their social network analysis maps to notice, wonder, and question how to enhance student connectivity to facilitate deeper learning. As we know, students who feel connected to their peers/classrooms/teachers are more motivated to learn (Carolan, 2013; DeLay et al., 2016; Maroulis & Gomez, 2008; Ryabov, 2011). This information will enable teachers to comprehend the social dynamics of their classroom, empowering them to make thoughtful decisions on fostering more inclusive and welcoming academic communities.

Below we provide a roadmap of how this book is organized. We encourage teachers to use the book as a resource for their own understanding of their classroom's social network maps, and to identify innovative ways of including children with different abilities and strengths across the school day.

Chapter 1 begins with an exploration of the significance of students' relationships. Subsequently, we examine the significance of inclusive education and practices, offering a definition of RI. Lastly, given the foundation of RI in a social network perspective, we present a summary of how social network analysis aids educators in comprehending and enhancing RI.

In Chapter 2, we define Research Practice Partnerships (RPPs) and how they previously have been used in school districts. We share lessons that we learned about how to develop and sustain a successful, mutually beneficial RPP between researchers and educators. We then describe our own RPP model that spawned the development of this book and include specific features of our RPP that supported our partnership. In particular, we describe how researchers and practitioners worked together to build meaningful friendship networks in the classrooms of the teachers with whom we worked. We also use this chapter to describe how we have extended our RPP model into this book for educators who may not have access to responsive education researchers and who want to try out, and engage with research tools to support their pedagogy.

In Chapter 3, we describe the SNA Toolkit and how teachers can use it to build a nurturing classroom community. We guide the reader through specific functions of the program and how to access the research tools. There is a lot of detail describing each step to access the program, including how to set up an account and how to obtain the protocols for educators to use with their students in their classrooms. Dr. Mamas has also kindly agreed to share a free "key" for readers of this book to access the tool and the online resources. This chapter also includes specific steps for how to interpret the data should teachers decide to use the SNA Toolkit. There are step-by-step instructions for how to make sense of the social network maps, including instructions for deciphering certain data within the maps and ideas for when and how to use the maps. Specific scenarios are also offered on how teachers can use the SNA Toolkit within their classrooms.

In Chapters 4 to 7, we discuss each of the aspects of RI by focusing on one of the questions we use in the SNA Toolkit. The focus questions are:

Chapter 4: Who Are Your Friends?
Chapter 5: Whom Do You Play with at Recess?
Chapter 6: Whom Do You Go to for Help with Your Classwork?
Chapter 7: Whom Do Talk to If You Are Having a Bad Day?

In each of these chapters, we provide specific classroom activities and vignettes that can be used by readers to foster relational inclusivity in their classroom communities. Building upon the scenarios provided in Chapter 3 regarding how and when to use the results of the Social Network Maps, one part of each chapter includes a description of the experiences that local classroom teachers had when they used the SNA Toolkit in their classrooms. We interpret this data using the process described in Chapter 3 and discuss classroom (and schoolwide) activities and structures to support teachers in strengthening and deepening relational networks in the classroom. Another part of these chapters provides teacher interviews, reflective questions, and detailed classroom vignettes with actual scenarios describing how teachers used the SNA Toolkit to promote the formation of strong, nurturing ties among the students in the classroom.

In Chapter 8, we summarize the "big ideas" presented in the book. We offer some suggestions for building on the work and research described in the previous chapters. We also provide some reflections from the authors and the teachers we worked with. Ultimately, this chapter lays the groundwork for deepening and expanding the RPPs, inclusive practices, and SNA analysis tools that build friendship networks and RI in the classroom.

We invite educators to use this book in ways that make sense for them. The book might serve as the subject of a professional book club or professional learning workshops. Grade level teams or mixed grade level groups could use the book to think together about how they might address a particular challenging student behavior or pedagogical practice. It might also be part of a larger focus on social-emotional learning. Regardless of how it is used, we hope the book allows educators to take a deeper and more focused look at student social networks and connections that exist within classrooms. We encourage educators, armed with this information, to build on existing strengths and connections to foster RI and a sense of belonging that will serve all students.

1

The Case for Relational Inclusivity

In the current educational landscape an essential paradigm shift exists that requires the attention of educators, parents, and policymakers alike: the profound significance of inclusive education and inclusive practices. In this transformative landscape, the ethos of acceptance, understanding, and support have become the cornerstones upon which a truly equitable and nurturing learning environment is built. But within the mosaic of inclusivity lies a concept often overlooked, an intricate thread that weaves the fabric of social relationships among elementary school students: *Relational Inclusivity* (RI). This term, illuminated by the lens of a social network perspective, delves deeply into the complex web of connections, friendships, and alliances that form the backbone of a child's educational journey. As we embark on this exploration, we are compelled to unravel the complexities of these relationships, understanding not just the individuals involved, but the ties that bind them and the transformative power they hold within the education system. This chapter begins by discussing the importance of students' relationships. Then we explore the importance of inclusive education and inclusive practices and provide a definition of RI. Finally, as RI is grounded in a social network perspective, we provide an overview of how social network analysis helps educators understand and transform RI.

DOI: 10.4324/9781003398738-1

The Importance of Students' Relationships

Relationships are fundamental to human well-being and have a profound impact on various aspects of our lives. They play a crucial role in enhancing our overall quality of life and contributing to our physical, emotional, and psychological health throughout life (Tay et al., 2013; Tian et al., 2014; Umberson et al., 2010). Strong social relationships and connections have even been linked to increased life expectancy. On the one hand, people who have meaningful relationships tend to lead healthier lifestyles and are more likely to adopt positive habits, such as exercising regularly, eating well, and avoiding harmful behaviors (Yang et al., 2016). On the other hand, social isolation has been shown to increase the risk of heart disease and stroke (Smith et al., 2021).

Social relationships play a particularly pivotal role in the overall development and well-being of elementary school students. During elementary school, children are not only acquiring academic skills but are also developing their social and emotional skills. Research has consistently highlighted the importance of social interactions and connections in fostering cognitive, emotional, and behavioral growth. Social relationships foster cognitive development in elementary school students. According to sociocultural theory, interactions with peers and more knowledgeable individuals facilitate the process of "scaffolding," wherein students are supported in their learning beyond their current capabilities (Vygotsky & Cole, 1978). Collaborative activities and discussions with peers stimulate critical thinking, problem-solving, and the exchange of ideas (Gokhale, 2012). According to Rogoff (1990), children's thinking and development are supported and grow in the immediate social contexts in which children are involved in problem solving, in collaboration with others or in social arrangements of children's activities. This connection to learning and academic success justifies dedicating time and attention to fostering social relationships within classrooms.

Positive social relationships are instrumental in promoting the emotional well-being among school students. Strong social connections and friendships can act as a buffer against the negative effects of stress and anxiety (Berndt & Keefe, 1995; Jones et al., 2017). Children's friendships, in particular, are closely associated with children's positive well-being. Engaging in friendships and experiencing a sense of belonging enhances self-esteem, self-concept, and overall emotional resilience (Holder & Coleman, 2015). According to Holder and Coleman (2015), "the establishment of intimate friendships begins in childhood and comprises an important landmark in development" (p. 81). Therefore it is important for educators to invest in creating the necessary conditions for friendships among their students to grow and thrive.

Elementary school is also a crucial period for acquiring essential social skills that are foundational for later life. Interacting with friends and peers helps students understand social norms, practice communication, and learn conflict resolution (Ladd, 2017). These skills are critical for successful interpersonal relationships and collaboration in both academic and real-world settings. Peer social relationships as well as relationships with parents and teachers can positively impact academic achievement. Positive relationships can predict good academic performance, while those ridden with conflict can predict poor academic performance (Yu et al., 2023). Cooperative group activities and discussions enable students to learn from each other's perspectives and develop a deeper understanding of subject matter (Slavin, 2014). Collaborative learning and peer interactions also lead to improved comprehension, retention, and motivation (Slavin, 2015). Educators, especially classroom teachers, have powerful opportunities to structure lessons and experiences to facilitate student-to-student connections and relationships which affect both academic and socio-emotional outcomes.

Furthermore, elementary school is a period of identity formation, where children begin to develop a sense of self in relation to their social environment. Interactions with peers allow students to explore their interests, hobbies, and personal strengths, shaping their emerging identities (Erikson, 1968). Friendships also play a role in helping children understand diverse cultural backgrounds and perspectives (Aboud & Doyle, 1996). When children make friends from diverse cultures, races, and backgrounds, they are more likely to develop understanding and respect for diverse cultural customs, traditions, and beliefs. This can enable children to be more accepting and respectful of diversity, as well as experience and perceive the world from multiple perspectives.

Engaging in healthy and meaningful social relationships has also been associated with lower rates of chronic illnesses, depression, anxiety, and other mental health issues (Holt-Lunstad, 2022). The emotional support and companionship provided by relationships contribute to better emotional resilience and coping skills as well as stress reduction (Ozbay et al., 2007). Additionally, having a network of supportive relationships can help minimize stress. Sharing experiences, talking about concerns, and receiving emotional support from loved ones can reduce the impact of stress on the body and mind (Alvord et al., 2021).

Social relationships hold immense significance for all school students, impacting various facets of their development. Cognitive growth, emotional well-being, social skills acquisition, academic achievement, identity formation, and intercultural understanding are all enriched through positive interactions with peers. Educators, parents, and policymakers should recognize the pivotal role of social relationships in education, and provide opportunities for students to cultivate meaningful connections that contribute to their holistic development. Healthy social relationships contribute to a fulfilling and meaningful life. The importance of fostering friendships and positive relationships within the elementary school context cannot be overstated.

Redefining Inclusive Education and Inclusive Practices

Inclusion is arguably a highly contentious term (Artiles et al., 2006; Mamas, 2013; McLeskey et al., 1998). The meaning of "inclusion" is by no means clear and perhaps conveniently blurs the edges of social policy with a feel-good rhetoric that no one could be opposed to (Armstrong et al., 2011). One may argue that inclusion was officially introduced by the Salamanca Statement (UNESCO, 1994) which is supported by a Framework for Action.

This Framework called for education systems to become inclusive by catering to diversity and special needs, and for schools to implement child-centered pedagogies in supporting all children. Florian (2008) defined inclusion in terms of a philosophy of education that promotes the education of all students in mainstream schools, and as a policy which is generally understood around the world as part of a human rights agenda that demands access to, and equity in, education (Florian et al., 2016). Artiles and colleagues (2006) argue that one of the most important developments in special education is the inclusive education movement, and conclude that inclusive education is necessary to achieve social justice for all students, especially those with disabilities and other marginalized identities.

Over the last several decades, students with disabilities have spent increasingly more time included in general education settings. In the US, in 1989, 31.6% of students with disabilities were educated in general education settings for over 80% of their school day. In 2017, this number had more than doubled with over 63% of students with disabilities being educated in general education settings for the majority of their school day (Snyder et al., 2019), and this number continues to grow to date. The increasing prevalence of students with disabilities in schools and classrooms supports a need for broader awareness and understanding of the strengths, attributes, and needs of these children, along with a focus on developing pedagogical tools and strategies to meaningfully include children with disabilities in these mainstream learning environments. Also, the growing awareness of cultural and linguistic diversity necessitates a broader look at inclusive practices.

A key element to enhancing inclusion is implementing inclusive pedagogy and inclusive education practices. Inclusive pedagogy—the way that classroom environments, activities, and assessments are designed to promote meaningful, relevant, and accessible learning for all students—has been developed as a response to the provision of a meaningful "education for all" (Florian & Black-Hawkins, 2011; Florian & Linklater, 2010). Diverse and minoritized students, especially students with labeled disabilities, are particularly vulnerable to exclusion from the culture, curriculum, and community of general education schools because of the deterministic beliefs and practices (i.e., beliefs and practices of ability labeling and ability-focused teaching) that guide many schools (Florian, 2013; Hart, 2004). Florian and Black-Hawkins (2011) conceptualized inclusive pedagogy as extending what is ordinarily available in the community of the classroom as a way of reducing the need to mark some learners as different. This conceptualization is supported by a shift in pedagogical thinking from an approach that works for most learners existing alongside something "additional" or "different" for those (some) who experience difficulties, towards one that involves providing rich learning opportunities that are available for everyone, so that all learners are able to participate in routine, classroom activities (Florian & Black-Hawkins, 2011, p. 826). The ultimate goal of inclusive pedagogical practice is to raise the achievement and success of all students (ESSA, 2015; Weiner, 2003) and, at the same time, ensure the inclusion of those who are vulnerable to exclusion and other forms of marginalization.

According to Florian and Black-Hawkins (2011, p. 818), three main assumptions are required for successful inclusive pedagogy:

1. A shift in focus from one that is concerned with only those individuals who have been identified as having "additional needs," to learning for all — the idea of everybody (not most and some)
2. Rejection of deterministic beliefs about ability (and the associated idea that the presence of some will hold back the progress of others)
3. Ways of working with and through other adults that respect the dignity of learners as full members of the classroom community.

These assumptions underpinned our research-practice partnership model.

Educators who implement inclusive practices to support ALL learners will likely have students who are more engaged and interested in the course content (Florian & Black-Hawkins, 2011;

Mamas et al., 2020). Many educators who strive to implement inclusive practices in their classrooms report that they find it challenging, due to lack of training, time, expertise, and tools (Mamas et al., 2019). Although teachers have the opportunity to collaborate with colleagues and fellow teachers to think about how lessons and activities could be inclusive, they have fewer opportunities to collaborate with researchers to learn and develop the latest research-based practices to support effective inclusion in their classrooms. This book addresses this gap by providing educators with a social network analysis toolkit and assorted activities to enable them to explore, understand, and enhance relational inclusivity within their classrooms. We now turn to defining and discussing the concept of RI in the wider context of inclusive education.

Relational Inclusivity Meets Inclusive Education

This book enables educators to pay close attention to social relationships by introducing and endorsing the concept of RI in the context of inclusive education. The goal of inclusive access for ALL learners is boosted when all learners have access and connections to each other. Grounded in the social network perspective, RI reflects the extent to which all students are appropriately engaged across crucial social dimensions of schooling. Drawing from our prior work (Mamas & Trautman, 2023; Mamas & Trautman, in press; Mamas et al., in press), we pinpoint four core networks that encapsulate the majority of students' functional social interactions at school:

- ◆ Friendship networks
- ◆ Recess/play networks
- ◆ Academic support networks
- ◆ Emotional well-being networks

These dimensions/networks serve as vital indicators, revealing the complex web of relationships that define a child's educational experience.

RI distinguishes itself from the concept of social participation (Koster et al., 2009, 2010), which typically emphasizes
friendships, relationship quality, and interactional behaviors
within theoretical frameworks. Unlike the broader notion of
belonging, which encompasses teacher-student relationships and
feelings of acceptance, <u>RI specifically examines concrete social
relationships between students across diverse domains</u>. Rather
than focusing solely on the sense of belonging, RI delves into the
active and reciprocal participation of students in relationships. It
offers a nuanced perspective, acknowledging that the concept of
"appropriate engagement" varies for each student. Recognizing
this diversity of relationships across students, RI employs practical measurement techniques through the SNA Toolkit, enab-
ling educators to identify patterns of engagement, comprehend
them, and intervene when necessary to disrupt troubling social
dynamics, such as isolation or potential bullying behaviors.

What makes RI compelling is its practical applicability within
the classroom, independent of overarching educational policies
and structures. It empowers teachers and educators to advocate
for inclusive practices and justice, ensuring that all students,
regardless of their differences in race, class, gender, ability, or
sexuality, are included. We recognize that SPED and linguistic-
ally and racially/ethnically diverse students often bear the brunt
of exclusionary practices, making it imperative to concentrate our
efforts on dismantling barriers and fostering inclusivity within
their social interactions (Mamas & Trautman, 2023). By acknowledging and paying attention to the strengths and connections of
marginalized students, we employ the tenets of inclusive education and enhance RI of all students.

Using Social Network Analysis

Social network analysis can help educators examine relational
inclusivity. Social network analysis focuses on two main aspects
(Borgatti et al., 2018):

1. Understanding how a network is structured
2. Figuring out the position of each person or entity within
   that network.

For example, in a classroom, the structure of the network (how students are connected to each other) is crucial for improving how teaching and learning happen there. Also, looking at where each student stands within this network can tell us a lot about the teaching and learning dynamics. What is even more important is that the way the network is set up and where people are positioned affects how resources and learning opportunities flow through the classroom, mainly through their relationships with each other.

Examining students' social networks in classrooms is a fundamental aspect of RI. A social network is a way of understanding how people or things are connected within a social system. Imagine it as a web of relationships among the various parts of the system. These parts can be thought of as "actors" or "nodes." These actors are the individuals or entities that make up the social network, such as students or teachers. The connections or "ties" between these actors represent the relationships they have with each other, like being friends, collaborating on projects, or seeking help from one another.

Another important aspect of social networks is the characteristics or attributes of the individuals or entities involved. These attributes can include things like gender, socioeconomic status, age, disability status, and more. Gathering this information, known as demographic or attributional data, can be crucial in understanding RI for historically marginalized groups of students. For instance, a teacher might want to compare how students with designated Individualized Education Programs (IEPs) are positioned within the social network compared to their non-IEP peers. Similarly, a teacher might be interested in examining how students who are chronically absent fare in their classroom's social networks.

Social network analysis has become more popular in recent years because of new tools being developed, as well as advancements in computational social sciences that make it easier to understand complex social networks quickly and with interesting, visually appealing maps. While social network analysis has started to be used in education research to study how young people interact, there are few studies that actively engage teachers as research partners to co-design both the social network mapping tool, and the classroom lessons and activities to support relational inclusivity in the classroom. This book introduces our reader partners to the SNA Toolkit, a tool co-developed with researchers and teachers that aims to provide teachers with an accessible platform to study their students' social networks and work together with their colleagues to develop lessons and activities that promote relational inclusivity in their schools and classrooms.

When we study social networks in the field of education, the actors or nodes are typically students and teachers. However, they can also include larger entities like classrooms, entire schools, school districts, or even entire countries. In the context of this book, our main focus is on studying social networks within elementary school classrooms. We are particularly interested in understanding how students interact with their peers. Therefore, we consider the classroom as the fundamental unit of analysis. It serves as the boundary for our study of RI.

In this book, our main focus is on grasping the structure of an entire classroom network and the positions of its members (students), within this social system. We adopt a "whole-network" approach, which means we aim to use a comprehensive set of network concepts and methods that assume we have access to the complete network. In the whole network approach, researchers or educators choose a group of nodes (in this case, students) as the population to study. For instance, all students within a specific classroom might be asked to identify whom they interact with in a particular way, like being friends with or playing with during recess. Consequently, the classroom serves as a sort of boundary for the network, and interactions outside the classroom are not considered. While this approach has limitations because it may overlook important connections outside the bounds of the classroom, it is adopted in this book because students typically spend a significant amount of time with their classmates, especially in elementary school. The classroom is also seen as a physical and pedagogical space where teachers can intervene, plan and implement educational activities to enhance the RI of their students.

Summary

In this chapter, we have discussed the significance of inclusive education and social relationships in the lives of elementary school students. From cognitive development to emotional well-being, from academic achievement to identity formation, these relationships are the cornerstone of holistic development during this crucial period of a child's life. We have emphasized the pivotal role that educators can play in nurturing and facilitating these connections. Furthermore, we have introduced the concept of RI from a social network perspective as a powerful way to better understand and improve these social relationships within the classroom setting. RI, grounded in social network analysis, provides a unique lens through which we can examine how students are interconnected, identify key individuals within the network, and explore how resources and learning opportunities flow through these relationships. As we move forward in this book, we will explore the practical application of SNA in the educational context. Our goal is to equip educators with the knowledge and tools to assess and enhance the RI of their students. By studying social networks within the classroom, we can gain valuable insights that can lead to more inclusive and supportive learning environments.

2

Research Practice Partnerships in Classrooms

Chapter 1 showed that inclusion has significant positive impacts on all children. Students benefit both academically and socioemotionally when the classroom environment supports inclusion. More importantly, the research tells us that all students are served when teachers deliberately and strategically employ effective inclusive practices in their classrooms. Teachers can have a positive impact on friendship networks within their classrooms when armed with useful information and effective friendship building activities.

Building on the research examining effective inclusive practices and friendship networks, this book came about as a result of a 2018 research grant in which we partnered with nine local classroom teachers in grades 3 through 8 to better understand how teachers think about inclusive practices, and support peer relationships in their classrooms. The teacher participants came from three different districts (four different public and/ or charter schools) across a large Southern California County. Students requiring free and reduced lunch ranged from 18% of the students to 99% of the students across all four schools. Classrooms included grades 3 through 8 in single subject classrooms, classrooms with block scheduling, and multiple subject self-contained classrooms.

DOI: 10.4324/9781003398738-2

Teachers ranged in their levels of teaching experience (3 to 17 years) and in their credential certifications. All participating teachers held multiple subject credentials. Some also had single subject authorizations and bilingual teaching credentials. Teachers' race and ethnicity were reflective of our state's racial and ethnic variability. Three teachers reported identifying as White, three teachers as Asian, one teacher as Black or African American, and two teachers as Hispanic. We wanted a diverse group of teachers and students to ensure that the project was accessible and relevant to a wide range of practitioners.

We came to the table with strong research backgrounds in special education, social network analysis, and elementary teacher education. The teachers came to the table with a wealth of "on the ground" experience, practical skills, and deep knowledge of their students. This defined our Research Practice Partnership (RPP). We recognized that researchers and practitioners have complementary and overlapping skills and interests. We took the best of what we all knew and could do, and we created a non-hierarchical environment that fostered an exchange of information and ideas. This RPP model shaped how we worked together, and it also informs the way we think about this book. We seek to provide research and relevant classroom activities that invite teachers to participate and actively engage with these resources in their own classrooms. We also offer the online SNA Toolkit for collecting friendship and other network data in the classroom.

Ideally, an RPP brings researchers and educators together to collectively solve pressing pedagogical problems. RPPs are considered an important and practical way for educators to use research to develop effective educational tools and classroom strategies (Coburn & Penuel, 2016; Estabrooks et al., 2019). RPPs may take many forms including research alliances, design research partnerships, and networked improvement communities (NICs), or any combination of these (Henrick et al., 2017). RPPs can support educators and researchers to address a problem of practice such as supporting teachers to meaningfully include individuals with disabilities in their general education classrooms. This book uses the RPP model to focus specifically on friendship networks and RI.

What Are the Essential Foundations of Our RPP Work and How Do They Apply to This Book?

In our work with the teacher team, we identified five key elements. Each element contributed to the collaborative relationship between researchers and practitioners. The elements also worked together to support teachers in meaningfully including ALL students. These elements lent themselves to innovations and "on the spot" adjustments as the collaboration progressed. Driven by the goals of the project and the needs and interests of the participants, these elements provided a framework for the RPP and can be adapted to specific content and anchor experiences.

1. An explicit, shared understanding of inclusive practices and inclusive pedagogy

Through readings, mini-lectures, lesson planning, and discussions, a deepening understanding of "inclusive pedagogy" evolved. Similarly, this book provides participants (readers) with a research background, classroom activities, and teacher reflections.

2. Anchor experiences and lessons that participants can refer to throughout the project

In our initial RPP, all participants watched a documentary, however, any number of anchor experiences could serve the same purpose. A journal article, a children's book, a news report, or "TED-like" talk might also become the common initial experience that researchers and practitioners can refer to throughout the project. This book itself might be considered the anchor experience, and we believe that all teachers who read it will similarly benefit from a shared experience and common foundational understandings. We encourage readers to take on this project with at least one other colleague in order to benefit from the collaborative professional learning opportunities the SNA Toolkit and the lessons offer.

3. An iterative process of meeting, discussing, assessing, co-planning

We held workshops that occurred throughout the school year so that participating teachers could share their experiences, apply new knowledge, and reflect on successes and challenges over the academic year. Chapters 4, 5, 6, and 7 provide readers/participants with multiple visits inside teachers' classrooms to learn a variety of inclusive practices and activities. The book also provides ongoing support for using the online SNA Toolkit.

4. A strengths-based approach to work with all students in the classroom

Adhering to the tenets of inclusive pedagogy, we approached the work with the understanding that all students are contributing members of the classroom community and everyone needs to be included in classroom activities. This philosophy underlies all aspects of the book's content.

5. A respectful, open disposition toward all questions and suggestions

An appreciation for the contributions and importance of both researchers and practitioners lay at the foundation of our work and discussions. We understood that we had much to learn from each other.

An ongoing feature of the RPP was the integration of SNA maps and the information they provided about friendship networks and RI in the participating teachers' classrooms. In particular, four network maps for each classroom were developed and presented by the researchers, as a direct result of the four student social network survey questions. These same four questions are used in this book to help collect data and organize classroom activities. While very accessible to the students, the questions yield deep and meaningful information about friendship networks and what Relational Inclusivity looks like in the classroom. These same four questions appear as chapter topics in this book. The questions are:

1. Who are your friends in the classroom? (Friendship Network)
2. Whom do you play/hang out with during recess? (Recess/Hangout Network)

3. If your teacher is not available, whom do you turn to for help on academic work? (Help Network)
4. Whom do you talk to if you are having a bad day at school? (Bad Day Network).

Our RPP provided a supportive community for teachers to try out ideas and learn from each other, and for researchers to share data that informed classroom lesson development. We co-developed research-based classroom lessons that were meant to encourage meaningful friendships and empower upper elementary school and middle school students to build strong social connections with their classroom peers, including those peers with disabilities. This iterative process of collaboration, innovation, and discovery can be adapted and used to address any urgent pedagogical problem where researchers and educators are willing to work together to support their own learning. The past few years taught us that a partnership does not necessarily require synchronous meetings with everyone in the same place. Communities of research and practice can occur across spaces and time. We hope that this book provides an anchor for such work.

While RPPs are one of the few ways that researchers can meaningfully support teachers to address urgent problems of practice, they are also not sustainable without the commitment of a researcher and a practitioner solving a problem together. We know that many teachers do not have easy access to education researchers and may not have the tools or the resources to engage in active, meaningful RPPs with researchers. With this book we will share useful, research-based tools that teachers can add to their toolkit to engage in their own research. In a sense, the SNA Toolkit and its accessible technology create an RPP environment for our readers. We participate with educators by sharing research, tools, activities, and strategies. We also use the book to provide vignettes and reflections from our teacher-colleagues, along with descriptions of how they used the SNA maps and activities in their own classrooms. We initially used the RPP model to develop a community of practice within a Southern California community to support educators and researchers in implementing relational inclusive pedagogy and practices in

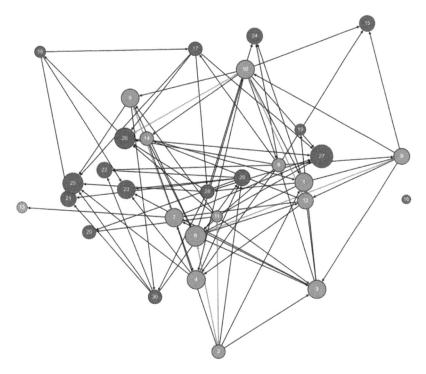

FIGURE 2.1 Friendship Network Map Beginning of Year

general education classrooms. With this book we aim to support the work more broadly.

As part of our RPP, teachers collected data in their classrooms and during the workshops, teachers were presented with their classroom's social network maps. Figure 2.1 shows one of the classroom friendship maps early in the year. Girls are shown in black circles and boys in gray. Light gray arrows show a reciprocal friendship nomination, whereas the size of nodes/circles is based on in-degree centrality, meaning the more nominations received by a student the bigger their circle.

Friendship Network Map Beginning of Year

In Chapter 3 readers will learn more details about the research tool and will have free access to it. Teachers can use it in their classrooms, along with the classroom strategies, activities, and ideas included in this book, to enhance relational inclusion in their classrooms. We will share the SNA Toolkit, developed by Christoforos Mamas (a co-author), and his colleagues. We invite teachers to try this tool in their classroom and support teachers to implement such tools. Readers of this book are encouraged to test out the SNA surveys, try them out in their classrooms, and let us know how (or if) it supports the development of RI and a stronger classroom climate. In this way, our work together offers an expanded view of RPPs and a hopeful model for growth of this approach.

What Did We Learn from Our Friendship Network RPP and How Does It Inform This Book?

In this book, we expand on the model and the findings from our previous RPP. Working with a diverse group of teachers who had different student populations was an important element of our RPP. We developed structured and semi-structured activities within a series of workshops over one academic year that exposed teacher participants and researchers to new ways of thinking about inclusive practices and social relationships in the classroom. We wanted to assess how this RPP approach fared across a wide range of classrooms, teaching styles, and grades. We also wanted to provide opportunities for teachers to hear from each other about how lessons and activities were implemented in different classroom settings. After each workshop, teachers tested new ideas, lesson plans, and strategies in their classrooms and made note of their students' engagement and learning outcomes. At the next workshop, we reflected upon teachers' observations and edited lesson plans and activities to more effectively support students.

Our group met four times during the school year. The three-hour workshops included meals and snacks and were held at the university after school hours, during the week. Each workshop had a specific focus and structure that allowed for scaffolded learning and reflective cycles of planning, teaching, and reflecting. The reflection focused on both activities implemented in the classrooms and data collected by the researchers.

As our work progressed, we realized the collaborative nature of the project informed both the work and the perspectives of all participants. Teachers learned how research was conducted, shared, and used to build curriculum and encourage social interactions between students. Researchers benefited from the "real world" experiences of classroom teachers and the "real time" approach to co-planning, co-reflection, and co-teaching activities implemented in the classrooms during the year. The workshop series allowed for a focused yet flexible workflow. Questions and ideas developed organically throughout the process, and participants had time to pursue answers over the course of the year. Ultimately, the model helped us identify some key factors that contributed to successful outcomes.

1. Meeting with each other throughout the year and sharing ideas and insights

Effective teacher development requires an interactive, respectful environment in which teachers have opportunities to learn from each other and engage in meaningful professional conversations. The participating teachers attended four meetings during the academic year. These structured meetings allowed for whole group and small group discussions, as well as school and grade level meeting time. We strongly encourage our readers to undertake the work with at least one colleague in order to replicate this aspect of the experience.

2. Tapping into the expertise of the researchers

Part of each meeting involved the researchers sharing their work and their research with the teachers. This aspect of the study resulted in a continuing cycle of teacher professional growth and understanding throughout the implementation. A key feature of this increased awareness and understanding manifested in the teachers' approaches to both the lesson planning and the social network analysis work. Similarly, Chapters 1 and 3 of this book offer the insights, tools, and data that relevant research provides.

3. Using a collaborative research-practitioner structure

Research shows that when addressing pedagogical problems of practice in schools, lasting changes occur when educators are involved in reforming practice with researchers (Handelzalts, 2009). The teacher and the researcher engage collectively as learners, collaborators, and innovators of change to solve the pedagogical problem of practice (Hujiboom et al., 2020). Our project put educators and researchers in the same room, working on the same project at the same time. Rather than having researchers tell teachers what to do, the teachers and researchers co-constructed the implementation plan and co-interpreted the research findings. This innovative structure proved mutually beneficial. The teachers deepened their understanding of and appreciation for the social network research methodology, while the researchers gained real-time, relevant data from the class-room teachers. The SNA Toolkit introduced in Chapter 3 gives readers direct access to a research-based instrument that will allow classroom teachers to gather and analyze data from their own classrooms.

4. Receiving relevant classroom data through the SNA protocol

The teachers used their SNA data in a variety of ways. Through the lens of inclusive practices, they could see which students in their class were connected to each other. They could also see "outlier" students and begin to address the social and emotional issues underlying students' limited social ties.

The teachers used the SNA data to plan lessons, think about strategic student groupings, and facilitate classroom discussions that support relational inclusion among all students in the class-room. The teachers found the SNA data and visuals "fascin-ating." One teacher explained:

> During the project we got to see the data related to the social networks in our classrooms displayed on a map. This helped my efforts to include more students because it made it obvious who was being included and who was left out. It was like a spotlight on something I hadn't taken enough time to focus on prior to this project."

We are delighted to share a tool that affords educators access to the often hidden element of friendship networks in the class-room. We will also share work and activities undertaken by teacher-colleagues who used the tool. During our initial RPP, teachers administered the survey three different times over the academic school year—before, during, and after lessons were implemented. The network maps were mainly used as a reflec-tion tool to identify students that might be at risk for exclu-sion, to think about appropriate student groupings for learning, and to stimulate discussion, questions, and reflection from teachers. For example, in the first network map we analyzed together, teachers realized that a student with an identified dis-ability barely had any friendship ties. Teachers discussed how to enhance the friendship ties of this student. They discussed classroom lesson ideas about how to include children in conversations, and how to invite students to play during free time. After such lessons had been implemented, survey two was conducted, which showed that the student had gained a number of friendship ties.

Educators using this book can choose to administer the survey to their students as many times as they deem useful. We recommend at least one initial survey, followed by a second survey later in the year after implementing some of the activities that support RI. Even using the survey once can provide insights into aspects of the classroom that are otherwise hidden.

5. Participating in a co-planning/co-teaching/co-reflecting protocol

Teachers grow professionally when they have opportunities to plan together. A large body of national and international research points to the benefits of the co-planning, co-teaching, co-reflecting cycle (Pratt et al., 2017). When teachers sit with each other and plan lessons together, they go beyond merely generating activities. They discuss the intricacies of teaching—questioning, grouping, supporting language—and more. The RPP project gave teachers the chance to plan together, then try the lessons, and come back to discuss the results. The richness of this cycle then informed subsequent lesson development. As one participating teacher put it:

"It was helpful to see examples and ideas from other teachers as a way to guide my instruction. While talking with teachers, I was able to discuss and read their reflections and then make the necessary modifications for my own classroom. Additionally, it was helpful to plan lessons together with teachers and talk through ideas.

As stated previously, we highly recommend using this book and the toolkit with at least one colleague in order to replicate the co-planning/teaching/reflecting cycle that proves so valuable to teachers in the classroom.

As a result of the workshop meetings throughout the year, teachers co-developed research-based lessons and activities that supported inclusive pedagogy in upper elementary and middle school classrooms. Overall, teachers reported a marked increase in confidence about their abilities to include all students. When asked how confident they were implementing class lessons that promoted inclusion, at the beginning of the RPP, teachers reported little to no confidence in their abilities to include all students in lessons focused on socio-emotional topics. At the end of the academic year, teacher participants reported confidence in their ability to include all students in the class lessons.

Our work generated new knowledge to transform traditional deficit perspectives historically used to view and educate children with disabilities into strength-based ideologies that supported the assets, strengths, and unique characteristics of ALL children and their different learning needs and abilities. The purpose of this partnership was to understand how teachers and researchers worked together to develop impactful lessons and activities to include all learners and build meaningful social relationships among the students in each classroom. Similarly, the purpose of this book is to provide teachers with appropriate tools and activities to enable them to enhance relational inclusivity in their classrooms.

We approached the project through an asset-oriented framework and took advantage of the diverse experiences of the participating teachers and their students. The teachers worked together in both mixed groups and grade level specific teams to develop detailed, student-centered lesson plans that met content and grade level standards. They also reflected on the lessons implemented, and used each other as sounding boards for ideas and lesson adaptations. Periodically researchers would observe teachers implementing lessons and activities in their classrooms, and make note of students' levels of engagement.

Collaborating researchers participated in all discussions and activities, contributing information and insights from their perspectives. Teacher surveys were collected at the end of the workshops. To measure student impact, we used social network surveys at three different time points over the academic year and student focus group interviews throughout the year. All classrooms showed significant growth in strengthening and deepening friendship network ties. We anticipate similar results for educators who use the resources within this book.

Summary

Research has shown that RPPs with actively involved teachers who engage in collaborative research design are more likely to make lasting education reform impacts (Handelzalts, 2009). Teachers' expertise—their years of experience implementing lessons and activities with diverse learners, their ability to collaborate with others, and their creativity—are essential skills to solve pressing educational problems within an RPP. We recognize that teachers have the background and experience to design activities that will likely be much more successful than the lessons and activities that researchers design alone. Researchers can design studies and tools to collect information regarding the classroom contexts, social relationships, and pedagogy to strengthen the classroom activities and lessons to promote inclusion. Bringing together the worlds of research and practice and leveraging the strengths of both in a collaborative context motivated us to write this book and continue the RPP journey.

3
The Social Network Analysis Toolkit

In this chapter, we describe the use of the Social Network Analysis (SNA) Toolkit to enable educators to understand and transform the social network dynamics within their classrooms. We understand that educators do not have the luxury to immerse themselves in RPPs due to various reasons, such as lack of time, availability of researchers, scarcity of resources, and others. To compensate for the availability of researchers, prerequisite knowledge, time, and resources, we propose the use of the SNA Toolkit which can be pivotal in compensating for researchers and their expertise. Any teacher can become an action researcher by making use of the SNA Toolkit without having any knowledge of social network analysis. The SNA Toolkit is an easy-to-use, web-based software that allows educators to more deeply explore student relationships in their classrooms. It was conceived, designed, and developed to enable educators to conduct basic and descriptive SNA research to understand the social network dynamics within their classrooms. A noteworthy advantage is that it does not require any knowledge around social network methods; the necessary elements are built into the software. Teachers only need their class rosters to set up the tool. The SNA Toolkit is currently hosted under the domain name Socionomy.net.

In the following sections, we guide the reader through some of the logistics and functions of the SNA Toolkit that can

DOI: 10.4324/9781003398738-3

be particularly useful for educators in examining the degree of Relational Inclusivity in their classrooms. Any educator can use the Toolkit to take a snapshot of the social dynamics within their classroom at a particular time point. The SNA Toolkit can be used across different grades with the use of age-appropriate prompts when collecting relational data from students. Educators can then gather analytics about the social relationships and networks of their students and inform their pedagogical decisions. For example, these analytics can help them streamline their seating arrangements or identify any students who may be at increased risk of social isolation and exclusion.

Specific Steps for Using the SNA Toolkit Online Program

At the classroom level, the teacher can use the SNA Toolkit to understand how students are connected within the classroom. In previous publications, we offered a detailed overview of the Toolkit and its utility (Mamas et al., 2019; Mamas & Huang, 2022). Here, we focus on presenting the basic steps and functions of how the Toolkit may be used to examine RI in the classroom. Below are specific steps teachers can follow to implement the Toolkit in their classroom. Relevant instructional videos are available on our website www.socionomy.net to guide you through the steps.

Step 1: Set Up an Account
Step 2: Create and Customize a Survey
Step 3: Disseminate the Survey to Students
Step 4: Look at the Survey Data
Step 5: Interpret the Data

Step 1 – Set Up an Account

First, any teacher who would like to use the SNA Toolkit should sign up by visiting the website www.socionomy. net and clicking on the "Teacher" tab. The sign-up process is fairly straightforward. The educator fills out the "Teacher Registration Form" (see Figure 3.1) so that they can set their login details. A registration key (provided for free with this book)

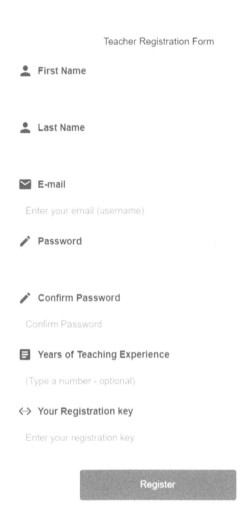

FIGURE 3.1 Teacher Registration Form

is needed to complete this step (please contact us via the contact form on our website, www.socionomy.net, to receive the registration key). Once this process has been completed, the educator has full access to the Toolkit's dashboard. This initial sign-up process should take a maximum of two minutes.

As part of step 1, the educator should "create" their classroom (see Figure 3.2). Educators can either manually add their students' names along with some demographic information (such as gender, disability status, race/ethnicity, etc.) or upload an Excel/CSV file with their students' names and demographic

Class Information

Class Name (please give your class a nickname):   Age Range of Students in this Class: School Year:

Choose An Option ⌄   2023/2024 ⌄

FIGURE 3.2 Creating a Classroom

information. A template Excel/CSV file is provided as part of the Toolkit to facilitate this process. It is worth noting that the initial classroom "creation" or registration happens one time only. An educator can add as many classrooms as they want. Students may be removed or added to reflect changes in classroom composition throughout the school year. If educators need assistance please send us an email with details of the issue to this email address: support@socionomy.net or complete a contact form on our website www.socionomy.net.

Step 2 – Create and Customize a Survey

After educators have created their classrooms, they can then populate a relational survey. Though the surveys are fully customizable, we recommend that the educators start with preprogrammed, suggested questions that reflect the four main RI aspects of this book. These four main survey questions include:

1. Who are your friends in the classroom? (Friendship Network)
2. Whom do you play/hang out with during recess? (Recess/Hangout Network)
3. If your teacher is not available, whom do you turn to for help on academic work? (Help Network)
4. Whom do you talk to if you are having a bad day at school? (Bad Day Network).

It is worth noting that questions may have a "tie strength" and a "frequency" component. Tie strength means that students can respond to the friendship network question by also answering the strength of their friendship ties with classmates. Once a student selects a classmate as their friend, the system then pops up three additional options and asks the student to pick how good of a friend their classmate is, ranging from very good friend to good friend to sort of a friend. These friendship tie strength variations can be set by the teacher on the Toolkit. The frequency component may ask the students to identify the frequency of the interaction during the play/recess network question. For example, they may say how often they play with a classmate, ranging from every day to once/twice a week to once/twice a month.

Educators may also choose to add to the survey any age-appropriate relational questions of interest to them or remove questions they do not wish to use. The survey can be deployed as many times as educators see fit for longitudinal data collection. Given that this data provides a "snapshot" of the RI within a classroom during one moment in time, it is valuable and preferable to collect these "snapshots" at multiple time points throughout the school year. This way, educators can track the progress of RI in their classrooms; they can identify where connections are plentiful and where they are non-existent or scarce. This formative assessment allows the teacher to develop class lessons and activities that mitigate the gaps in social connections or exploit the connections that are plentiful with associated class lessons and activities to promote interdisciplinary learning objectives. For example, educators may implement a lesson on the importance of friendship and collaboration among students.

Step 3 – Disseminate the Survey to Students

Educators will share a survey link with their students that is automatically generated by the SNA Toolkit. We recommend teachers spend time in class introducing the Toolkit and explaining its purpose to their students prior to administering the first survey. This introduction should be age appropriate. It's important for students to know that the surveys are private and only the teacher will look at the results to learn more about friendships in the classroom. For younger students, teachers may even want to examine the survey together as a class and talk about the questions they will be asked on the survey. Students then click on the link and respond to the survey. The first thing students have to do when they click on the link is to select their name from a dropdown list. The system is asking students to confirm that their selection is correct. As soon as a student selects their name from the list, then their name disappears from the list. Therefore making it easier for the other students to find and select their name on the list.

Step 4 – Look at the Survey Data

Upon completion of the survey, the Toolkit generates the results for the classroom. The results include both a classroom report and an individualized report for each student. Educators have immediate access to those results and reports with a click of a button. The results include visual network maps (sociograms) for the classroom social networks based on each prompt/question in the survey. For example, the friendship question will yield the friendship network map for the classroom. Figure 3.3 shows one such example network map. It should be noted that each student in the class has a unique ID number (shown on the network map) so teachers can easily see both the big picture and individual students.

After the data has been collected and the reports populated, educators at the classroom level must make sense of it. Each question's network map can be customized to highlight information of interest to the teacher, with options to change node size, color, and shape based on different measures and variables. In Figure 3.3, for example, each node (geometric shapes) represents a student in the classroom. The node size is based on the number of

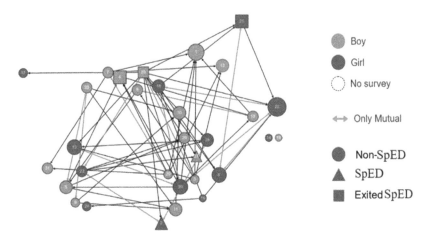

FIGURE 3.3 An Example of a Classroom Friendship Network Map

friendship nominations received from each student, or in-degree centrality (meaning that the more nominations received, the bigger the node size is). Alternatively, node size can be set to adjust according to other measures, such as out-degree centrality (number of nominations sent out by each student). In Figure 3.3, the different colors/grayscale shades show the gender of students. These color schemes can also be adjusted for any other demographic variables in the dataset. The triangular and square shapes represent students within the sphere of special education (students with IEPs or 504 Plans). In this case, triangular shapes show students with an IEP/504, the square-shapes represent students who have exited their special education program. Arrows indicate the friendship nominations made by each student, with light gray double-edged arrows showing mutual friendship nominations. If any student does not complete the survey, their node is shown with a dotted outline.

A picture is worth a thousand words. A social network map (Figure 3.3) represents a visualization of a classroom friendship network. It is what we call throughout the book a "snapshot" of the ties within the network of a particular classroom. In this section, we highlight a few noticings to start illustrating some of the questions and ideas educators might want to consider when engaging with the data. Chapters 4, 5, 6, and 7 focus on classroom lessons and strategies that address various aspects of the SNA snapshots.

The social network data in the map is a starting point for further investigation; analysis should prompt further questions. First, we look at students around the periphery of the map (see Figure 3.4).

For example, you may notice three students (14, 18, 19) with no incoming friendship nominations (as in, no one identified them as a friend). Of these, only one (19) identified other classmates as friends. Additionally, two other students (17, 24) have no outgoing nominations. Though none of these are students with disabilities, educators might want to dig into why these students were not identified as friends and why Students 17 and 24 did not identify any friends. A teacher may think about having one-on-one conversations with each of these students to

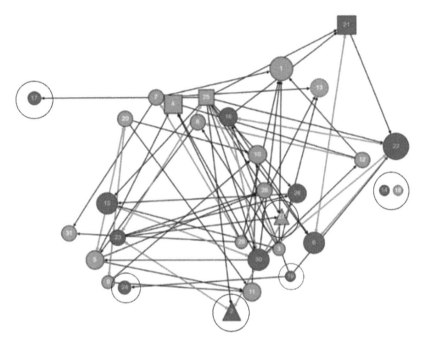

FIGURE 3.4 Understanding the Friendship Network Map

understand their social emotional needs and how the classroom context could be changed to address these needs. For example, four of these students identify as female. This might prompt educators to think specifically about the gendered dynamics of the classroom. Further, they may ask, what does their classroom engagement look like? What factors might be leading to their friendship isolation? Does this isolation extend into other networks in which they participate? Therefore, it is important to use the Toolkit to examine different networks that capture diverse domains of socioemotional and academic well-being of students. For example, friendship networks may be studied along with recess and academic help networks.

A second observation is that by and large, students with disabilities (2, 27) appear to be relatively well-connected to other students, with Student 2 having two reciprocal ties (light gray double-edged arrows) and 27 both giving and receiving friendship nominations. This might prompt educators to think about what aspects of the classroom community are contributing to this

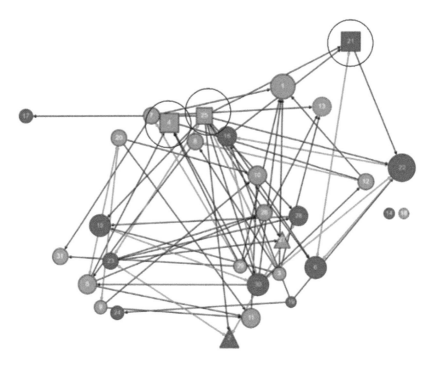

FIGURE 3.5 Understanding the Friendship Network Map Continued

dynamic. Insight into the teaching and social practices facilitating this RI merits further investigation. On a similar note, we notice that students who have exited special education (4, 21, 25) are similarly well-connected (see square shapes on Figure 3.5), with Student 25 appearing to be a hub of social activity, particularly in relation to outgoing nominations. It should be emphasized that the Toolkit should not be used exclusively to uncover what is "wrong" with RI but rather to share what works well in specific classrooms.

Our intention here is not to provide a "cheat sheet" as to what educators should be noticing on the various network maps of their respective classrooms. Instead, we see the Toolkit as a starting point for feedback and discussion on RI that is based on systematic data collection and evidence that can be made available quickly and at low cost. We encourage educators to be thoughtful and systematic with their observations. They should design and implement pedagogical activities that address the social needs and exploit the social strengths of the students in their classrooms. They should develop tailored activities that will serve the interests of their students, especially those who need the most support. In the following section, we provide some possible scenarios for how educators may use the SNA Toolkit to enhance RI within their classrooms.

Step 5 – Interpret the Data

In addition to examining the social network maps (sociograms), educators can explore descriptive SNA measures included in the classroom and student-level reports to help them better understand their students' social ties. The classroom report includes the density for each classroom network. Classroom network density shows the portion of the potential connections in a network that are actual connections, and it is represented by a percentage. For example, if the density within the friendship network of a classroom is 23%, that means that out of a possible 100 connections, 23 exist. If all students were connected to each other with a friendship tie (a very unlikely scenario), the density would be 100%. A low network density may be a sign of a sparsely connected classroom in which information, knowledge and resources may not transfer between people easily. Having the ability to compare and contrast these measures across different time points can be particularly useful for educators to track the progress of their students in terms of social engagement and RI. Additionally, the average degree centrality for each of the networks is provided in the classroom report. In the case of the friendship network, the average degree centrality would show how many friendship nominations were received or sent out on average by each student. For example, if the average degree centrality is seven, this would mean that on average each student in that classroom received or sent out seven friendship nominations. Lastly, at the dyad level, reciprocity is also calculated which is a measure that shows how many of the ties in the network are reciprocated. A higher number of reciprocal ties may be a sign of a close-knit classroom community with higher relational inclusivity.

Descriptive measures such as in-degree and out-degree centrality are also included in the student report. In-degree centrality shows the number of nominations received by each student. For example, in a friendship network, if the in-degree of Nicolas is three, that means that three of their classmates identified them as their friend. This measure can show how sought after a student is within each network in the classroom. On the flip side, out-degree centrality shows the outgoing nominations of a student. For example, if Nicolas identifies eight students in the classroom as their friend, their out-degree would be eight. Comparing in-degree and out-degree centrality for Nicolas, we may observe that he has more outgoing friendship nominations (8) than incoming (3), suggesting that this student may be over-estimating the nature and depth of their classroom relationships. Additional measures are anticipated to be included in future iterations of both the Toolkit's classroom and student reports, which are revised as additional educator feedback is collected, new insights in research emerge, and as technology advances.

How Can Educators Use the Toolkit

Based on the unique context of each classroom and the specific developmental needs and strengths of the students, it is up to the teacher to decide what they want to do with the SNA Toolkit and how they want to do it. Depending on when teachers administer the surveys and what questions they have about their classroom communities, the survey data can provide useful ways to inform teacher practice and facilitate greater Relational Inclusivity.

Scenario 1 – Start at Beginning of the School Year

Educators may use the SNA Toolkit at the beginning of the school year (a few weeks in) to get a "snapshot" of the initial/emerging social relationships among their students. Many educators apply academic formative assessments at the beginning of the year to see what their students know and what areas they need to grow in. In a similar manner, they can apply the Toolkit to explore early the social strengths and needs of their students. In this way, they can identify students early who may need additional social emotional support and identify students who might be "social butterflies" and who may act as relationship brokers in the class-room. Early identification is key in addressing challenges and making sure that students receive the support they need to stay socially engaged within the larger classroom and school com-munity. Another advantage of applying the Toolkit early is that it enables educators to capture a baseline reading of the social dynamics in their classrooms.

Baseline data can help educators devise more efficient seating plans (e.g., create groups based on social preference), implement ice-breaker activities so that students are given opportunities to interact with classmates that they do not typically interact with, and finally have a systematic data collection point to be able to compare back to as the year continues. As the school year goes on, teachers may implement activities, such as those described in the following chapters, to enhance the RI of their students. Taking two to three "snapshots" throughout the year with the SNA Toolkit can help teachers examine the effectiveness of those activ-ities and, if necessary, modify them. Finally, the pre-programmed relational survey that is administered via the SNA Toolkit consists of four main questions that collect information on four networks; friendship network, recess/hangout network, help network, and bad day network. We advocate for early examination of these four main networks as they may reveal areas for growth that the edu-cator may focus on throughout the year. For example, the results may show that students face additional challenges interacting during recess (recess/hangout network) and receiving academic support from classmates (help network). Knowing this early in the year can help educators focus their efforts in enhancing these two main aspects of RI. Teachers can implement some of the ideas and activities proposed in the respective chapters of this book, or devise their own activities to help their students grow their outside of classroom interactions (recess/hangout network) and their help-giving behaviors (help network).

Scenario 2 – Identify At-risk Students

Teachers can use the SNA Toolkit to identify students who are at a higher risk of social exclusion and marginalization. One powerful element of the Toolkit is that it can provide systematic data and information on the relational status of each student in the classroom. An individual student report is populated by the Toolkit outlining the relational status of each student. Research shows that particular groups of students, including students with disabilities, are more likely to be socially excluded. Students with disabilities have fewer friends and are less accepted by peers (Koster et al., 2009, 2010; Mamas et al., 2019; Rotheram-Fuller et al., 2010). They are also more likely to be on the periphery of their social networks, report poorer quality of friendships, and have fewer reciprocal friendships (Kasari et al., 2011). Oftentimes they also experience bullying, alienation, and exclusion (Qi & Ha, 2012; Van Mieghem et al., 2020). Relevant data collection and analysis through the Toolkit can identify those marginalized students more quickly and more clearly. In large and busy classrooms, it is hard for the teacher to decipher the social interactions and acceptance of each student by classmates. Without systematic data collection about the students' social interactions and friendships, some students may fall through the cracks and remain alienated and excluded if the classroom teacher is not aware of their situation. The first step in addressing a student's exclusion is knowing about it, and the Toolkit can provide teachers with that knowledge. Teachers can then implement activities and practices to address the relational needs of the students who are at higher risk of exclusion. For example, having a daily morning cycle meeting could help students enhance their sense of belonging to the classroom and share any concerns they may have in terms of their social and emotional needs.

Scenario 3 – Assess Pedagogical Activities

Another important use of the SNA Toolkit would be to assess the effectiveness of pedagogical activities aimed at addressing and enhancing RI. We provide vignettes and examples of recommended activities in chapters 4 to 7. For example, a teacher may identify issues with RI in their classroom and decide to address those. These issues may include a student being without any friendship or other ties, students with many outgoing ties but not any or very few incoming ties, students with "broken" ties (ties that existed in previous data collection and are no longer there), and others. They may use the Toolkit to get a "snapshot" of the social dynamics before the implementation of any activities and then use it again, after completing the activities, to ascertain the change in RI within their classroom. They would be able to see whether the implemented activities contributed to any gains in relational ties among their students as far as the four main social networks are concerned.

It should be noted that it is not necessary to assess all four classroom social networks (i.e., friendship, recess/hang out, help, talk) each time the network survey is administered. An educator may decide to focus on activities that promote recess interactions (recess network). In that case, they could apply the relational survey with just one question; whom do you play with during recess? It should only take a few minutes for children to fill out the survey with only one question. To sum up, the Toolkit may be used as a formative assessment tool to ascertain the efficacy of implemented pedagogical strategies to promote RI.

Scenario 4 – IEP Purposes

It is almost certain that each general elementary education classroom has students with disabilities, defined as those with an IEP or with a 504 plan. According to Kurth et al. (2021), an IEP is a written plan that helps children with disabilities receive personalized and specific assistance and allows them to receive special education or other resources needed to be more successful in school. Similarly, a 504 plan helps provide resources and support for children with disabilities that are not eligible for an IEP. Annual goals are a fundamental component of the IEP which include, in many cases, goals relating to a child's social or emotional needs. In addressing the annual goals, teachers need to collect and maintain systematic evidence and data to show that these goals have been met. It is here that the SNA Toolkit may be particularly useful for educators to enable them to collect, analyze, and store data and evidence on the social and emotional progress of their students with IEPs or 504 plans. Specifically, the individual student report can be extremely valuable for educators as a piece of evidence for their student's relational and socioemotional growth. The teacher may use the Toolkit to monitor student progress in regards to their stated IEP or 504 plan goals and be able to provide evidence for achieving those goals or not. For example, the individual student report shows the number of incoming and outgoing nominations the student received and sent, respectively. This evidence can show the change in relational ties between different data collection points and hence show if a student with an IEP has met their relational IEP goals.

Scenario 5 – Keep Families Informed

Increasingly parents are concerned about the social and emotional well-being of their children at school. How children get along with each other is something that is very important for parents, especially parents who have children with identified disabilities. The SNA Toolkit is a comprehensive way to keep parents and families informed about the social relationships and interactions of their children with their classmates. Teachers can share the individual student report with the families of the child during parent-teacher conferences or through electronic communications. The report can be stored on any computer as a .PDF document and can easily be printed out or emailed to parents. Having a systematic approach to measuring the individual RI of each student and the ability to share the findings with the child's parents could make a big difference in keeping parents informed about their child's well-being, friendship ties, or any other element of RI. Careful planning and clear intentions are essential for educators who decide to share data with families. When sharing with families, educators need to have deliberate plans and policies in order to maintain privacy and avoid comparisons or rankings of students. Educators should also ensure that all parents can have access to this information, irrespective of their linguistic, digital, and socioeconomic status.

Summary

This chapter represents our current thinking about the SNA Toolkit and its main functions, which are prone to change as we constantly update and improve it. At the end of the day, it is really up to the individual teacher to assess the unique needs of their students and decide how best to use the SNA Toolkit to enhance RI. We conclude this chapter by outlining some useful Dos and Don'ts for educators when using the SNA Toolkit.

Dos:

♦ Use the SNA Toolkit to explore the four dimensions of RI.
♦ Try to get all of your students to complete the survey.
♦ Repeat the survey at different times throughout the school year.
♦ Revise the survey to meet your classroom's unique needs.
♦ Follow up with activities described in this book and beyond to enhance the RI of your students.
♦ Respect the privacy of your students when sharing results with others.

Don'ts

♦ Don't ask negative survey questions that could be sensitive to some or all of your students. For instance, refrain from asking, "Whom do you not want to play with?"
♦ Don't treat the results from the survey as a "popularity" contest.
♦ Don't force your students to participate in the survey if they don't want to.
♦ Don't assume this is the full picture of your students' Relational Inclusivity. They may have friends and other contacts outside the bounds of the classroom.

4

Who Are Your Friends?

What the Research Tells Us

♦ Friendships have been shown to promote social-emotional competence and buffer against depression for pre-adolescents and adolescents.

♦ Friendships have been shown to predict a sense of belonging to school and improved academic outcomes for students from marginalized backgrounds.

♦ Friendships promote self-empowerment and self confidence among all youth.

Teachers know intuitively that secure, strong friendships promote positive social emotional and academic outcomes in classrooms. For children from marginalized backgrounds, friendships are a protective factor in supporting their sense of belonging in school (Delgado et al., 2016). Research shows that ethnically and racially diverse students who report having friendships with school peers also report a greater sense of belonging to school and higher academic achievement (Knifsend et al., 2018). Humans are social creatures and positive, supportive connections contribute to well-being and a sense of belonging—two vital aspects of a healthy and supportive classroom community. Teachers who spend time creating inclusive classroom

DOI: 10.4324/9781003398738-4

communities will likely have academically high achieving students who feel socially and emotionally supported.

A large body of research describes the importance of friendships for ethnically and ability diverse school-aged youth. Friendships have been found to support the social and emotional development of children and adolescents (Bagwell & Bukowski, 2018). In fact, friendship quality has been reported to protect against depressive symptoms for pre-adolescents (O'Connor et al., 2023) and is related to less loneliness (Schwartz-Mette et al., 2020). Researchers have also found a positive relationship between the size of youths' social networks and their sense of satisfaction and confidence (Ferguson et al., 2022). Youth with large social networks report more self-confidence.

All children benefit from having deep and meaningful friendships with peers. Adults can play a key role in supporting these connections, particularly in facilitating relationships between typically developing children and those identified as having more complex disabilities (Rosetti & Keenan, 2018). Given the positive impact of friendship on youth and the recognition that it may be more challenging for some children to form relationships, it is crucial for educators to monitor, support, and devote class time to facilitating the opportunities and skills students need to develop meaningful friendships.

Using the SNA Survey and Maps to Learn about Classroom Friendships

Teachers can use the SNA survey and resulting network maps or sociograms to learn more about what is going on in their classrooms. The maps reveal friendship networks and social dynamics that are not always visible in the classroom. Educators can use the maps to see who is connected to whom and to what degree. The tool and the data provide insights and more importantly, spark questions about the social dynamics in the classroom. What story does this map tell? How can I capitalize on the strong friendships that already exist in my classroom? In what ways might I facilitate friendship connections among students

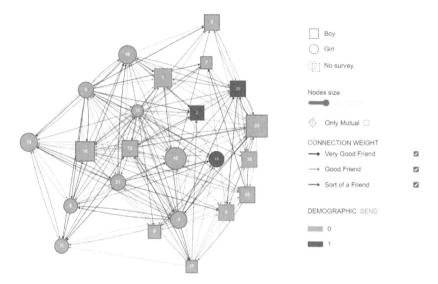

FIGURE 4.1 Friendship Network Map by SPED Status

who are less connected? The SNA Toolkit allows for systematic data collection which can then be applied to lesson plans and structures that capitalize on the data provided.

Figure 4.1 shows the friendship network and social ties that exist in a racially and ethnically diverse fifth-grade classroom with three students who have IEPs. The terms SPED (Special Education) and SEND (Special Educational Needs and Disabilities) are used interchangeably throughout the book. The boys are squares and the girls are circles. The size of each node indicates how many friendship nominations each student got from classmates who completed the survey. This is called in-degree centrality. This teacher was interested in seeing the overall friendship connections within the class. The teacher also wanted to understand how the SPED students (Students 2, 14, 20) were included. Susan noticed that overall her students were well-connected, as the map shows that all students nominated at least one other student as a friend. Student 2, a boy with an IEP, had relatively few nominations compared to most of his classmates.

From this map Susan could consider classroom structures and practices that may have helped or hindered friendship connections. She could also see whom Student 2 nominated as a friend and group those students together for collaborative learning activities. From conversations with the teacher, we learned that Susan decided to more closely observe Student 2's patterns of interactions with his peers during class time. She hoped her observations would help her pinpoint some concrete suggestions for how Student 2 could engage in more positive interactions with more classmates, which, in turn, could lead to more friendship ties. The SNA map proved useful in supporting the teacher's decisions about student groups and learning activities based on real data from her classroom.

When Christian, a third-grade teacher, saw his students' friendship map, he was not surprised that some of the students in his class had gotten many friendship nominations. He noted that these students were generally helpful and kind. Christian identified a few students who had not received many friendship nominations. He noticed that they were either students with IEPs or students who were chronically absent. (Christian added a demographic characteristic variable "chronically absent" to determine how connected these students were in his classroom). This information led Christian to wonder how he could incorporate these students more fully into the already existing friendship networks of the class.

Figure 4.2 shows the map of the same classroom with race/ethnicity (RE) as the demographic of interest. The teacher wanted to look at how RE might factor into friendship connections.

Student 16 is the only African American in the classroom. If the teacher was wondering how connected this student felt, the map would give a quick snapshot of whom this student nominated as friends and how this student connected with others. In this case the map shows that race did not seem to impact friendship nominations or ties for this particular student, because this student received and nominated multiple classmates as friends.

Nilu, a fourth-grade teacher in a diverse, under-resourced community noticed several things after her students completed their initial surveys. She was surprised that some of her most quiet students received lots of friendship nominations. She had assumed some of the louder, more boisterous students who tended to get a disproportionate amount of the teacher's attention were popular with their peers. Nilu noticed these students actually got few nominations. Nilu's observations prompted her to rethink

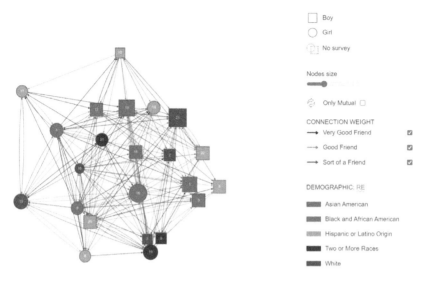

FIGURE 4.2 Friendship Network Map by Race/Ethnicity

some of her previous ideas about friendships within her classroom and the relationship between attention seeking behaviors and friendship ties. Another teacher, Adele, noticed that her multilingual learners who were pulled out for English support had strong friendship ties. She wondered if the friendships were bolstered by their shared pull-out experiences, their shared language, and/or other factors. These teacher wonderings can lead to a cycle of observation, small adaptations, more observation, and further questions. Over time, teachers find interventions and nuanced adjustments that build students' social skills and friendship ties.

Students' perceptions of who their friends are also plays an important factor in completing and interpreting the surveys. As one teacher noted, "It was interesting to see that each student did not see mutual connections." The teacher also observed that: "There were two students in my class who chose every student as a friend. They explained that they're friends with everyone." What are the implications for students who think they are friends with everyone but the connections are not mutual? What are the implications for students who don't realize that many of their classmates regard them as a friend? A thoughtful classroom teacher equipped with this knowledge can strategically plan to bring such students a greater sense of social awareness and work to provide them with the interpersonal tools to effectively engage with their classmates. In the next section of this chapter, we will examine classroom and schoolwide practices that can facilitate friendships and Relational Inclusivity.

Learning from the Students

In addition to using the SNA Toolkit and the social network maps to learn about the students, the survey itself offers an opportunity to learn *from* the students. As an introduction to the survey, we encourage educators to talk to students about friendship before they independently complete the survey. These discussions, which can happen during morning meetings, can serve as a formative assessment and provide the teacher with valuable information about how students define a friendship and how students think about their own friendships. These discussions also prepare students to be thoughtful and conscientious as they complete the survey. Susan, a sixth-grade teacher, led a brief discussion about friendship with her students before they took the survey. She wanted students to consider different types of friends and what makes a "very good" friend versus a "good" or "kind of" friend. One student explained:

> I think a very good friend is a friend that's kind of like me and Maya because we're always together at lunch and recess, and we're always buddies in class. But then another of my classmates, we're just friends in class, and when we're outside of class we don't really hang out as much.

Most third to sixth graders can complete the surveys independently on their laptops or tablets. We encourage teachers to find a bit of time to sit with some students while they take the survey and ask them questions. Short interviews with individual students during or after they take the survey also leads to deeper understanding of students' friendship networks and values. These brief one-on-one conversations can shine a light on individual students' feelings and interpersonal dynamics that are not always readily apparent to a busy teacher. The conversations can also yield interesting information about friendships and interactions within the classroom.

For example, a fourth grader, Sergio, was taking the survey, and we asked him how he was selecting his friends. Sergio offered very thoughtful criteria. He explained that he nominated friends based on how well he knew them, their personalities, and how they treat him. Valerie and Jason, on the other hand, based their nominations on how much time they spent with their friends and how much they talk together. PJ explained that he selected friends based on whom he played baseball with and whom he had known for a long time. Hortensia nominated her classmates based on how much fun they have together and how they help her. Not only do the surveys help us learn about friendship connections, they have the potential to help us learn how individual students define friendships.

Talking to the students about the survey also uncovers some of their social-emotional characteristics. Amir stated that he felt "a little sad" taking the survey because he had to say some of his classmates were better friends than others.

Explicit Instruction in Prosocial and Positive SEL Skills

Our work with teachers confirmed their wealth of professional knowledge. Teachers know and implement many activities and routines in order to create a positive classroom community. Using the additional information that the SNA surveys and maps provide, teachers can fine tune some of these activities and routines to foster deeper levels of Relational Inclusivity. Daily circles of 5 to 10 minutes over the course of a school year can lead to enormous growth in students' social-emotional learning (SEL). The content for the circle activities can include a quick game or an interesting question to understand students' perspectives about friendship. The circle discussions can include questions that promote students' friendship ties. Some of the questions teachers in our work have used are:

How are you feeling today? (Offer a scale or ways to describe feelings/mood such as weather, colors, etc.)

What makes someone a good friend?

Who has a kind word to say to someone who was a good friend today? (Offer sentence frames such as "Thank you _____ for being a good friend when you _____.")

How were you a good friend today?

Tell a story about when you stood up for yourself or someone else.

The Responsive Classroom[1] provides a wealth of resources for activities, structures, and discussion prompts, which can heighten students' awareness and ability to reflect on friendships.

Many teachers and schools use a Restorative Justice[2] approach to help students resolve interpersonal conflicts. Rather than focusing on negative behaviors and punishing the perpetrator, a restorative approach seeks to heal and connect. Teachers use a questioning protocol:

What happened?

What were you thinking of at the time?

What have you thought about since?

Who has been affected by what you have done? In what ways?

What do you think you need to do to make things right?

The restorative approach focuses on acknowledging, understanding, and addressing harm. Through the protocol, students become more self-aware and empathetic, leading them to tools for better friendship skills.

The CASEL Framework[3] identifies five competencies for social-emotional learning (SEL)—self-awareness, self-management, social awareness, relationship skills, and responsible decision-making. When students learn about these competencies and have opportunities to practice them, their SEL and relational skills improve. One way to help students become more self and socially aware is to explicitly teach listening skills. When analyzing her students' friendship maps, Adele noticed that one of her students had a relatively low number of friendship nominations. She commented, "He really struggles—he doesn't have a lot of social awareness. He's learning how to listen. He begins responding while the other child is talking." We know many students (and some adults) struggle to actively listen at a high level. They are more focused on waiting for their turn to talk or sharing a personal reaction to what the speaker said. A "fish-bowl" approach where the teacher and volunteer students "act out" different listening skills while the rest of the class watches can be effective. Students can critique what was effective and supportive in a low stakes context.

Business coach and author Steven Covey[4] identifies 5 Levels of Listening:

1. Ignoring
2. Pretend listening (Same as above)
3. Selective listening (Choosing what you want to hear)
4. Attentive listening (Repeating back what you've heard)
5. Empathic listening (Sharing the emotions you've heard)

Kathy, a third-grade teacher, uses these levels to help students build their self-awareness and also hone their social awareness. She introduces these levels of listening to her students, and structures listening practice sessions with pairs of students. Kathy might give a prompt such as, "Tell about a pet you want to have when you're older." Student A talks about their future pet for 1 minute without interruption. Student B tries to listen at Level 4 or Level 5. The students switch roles, then Kathy leads a discussion about how the experience was for both the speaker and the listener. She helps students identify the specific behaviors and actions that promote high level listening and empathy.

Mary, a SPED teacher, told us about the explicit relational behaviors she helps her students learn. These actions include turn taking, sharing, using language appropriately, and initiating connection. Mary explained that her students benefit from clear and consistent messages about their behaviors and interactions with others. It is the teacher's job to identify what types of support the students need and how best to prompt them toward the desired, positive behaviors. The hierarchy of prompts[5] assists teachers in considering the appropriate level of support for each student. The hierarchy also helps teachers move students toward more independence and agency.

We believe all students benefit from direct learning about friendships and prosocial behavior. And teachers can better assist students in expanding their friendship networks by informally assessing their needs and exposing them to the social cues and interpersonal skills that help them connect more effectively with their peers. Investing time in this type of work not only benefits individual students; it benefits the friendship ties among students and the classroom community as a whole.

Facilitating Activities That Maximize Engagement and Collaboration

Classrooms are intellectual communities. Teachers and students work together to investigate academic content and learn across the curriculum. While investing time in explicitly teaching SEL skills pays great dividends, teachers cannot invest all their time in SEL focused activities. High stakes testing and increasingly demanding academic expectations cause teachers to feel very pressured to focus on academic content. Many teachers we worked with expressed the frustration of wanting to spend more time on SEL and friendship building but not having the time or the support to do so. The good news is that teachers can facilitate friendship connections and RI throughout the school day. Maximizing student collaboration and communication within a lesson integrates SEL and friendship opportunities across the curriculum.

For example, Caren did a STEAM (Science, Technology, Engineering, Arts, Math) integrated activity with Nilu's fourth graders. The focus was an engineering/math challenge to build the tallest possible tower using only toothpicks and Play-Doh. The secondary goal was getting students to work together and communicate effectively with each other. (Caren did a similar lesson with Adele's fourth-grade class, substituting index cards and tape for the toothpicks and clay.)

After quick introductions on the rug, Caren began with a warm up activity, Count to 10. The object is to take turns counting up to 10, one person at a time, without interrupting. If there is an interruption or overlap in the counting, the group starts back at 1. Caren modeled the game with a few students, then groups of four or five played a few rounds. The students were very excited about the game, and Caren used the experience as a context for introducing the importance of listening carefully and paying attention to others' verbal and non-verbal messages.

Caren explained that the students were about to try an engineering challenge that would require the same skills. As seen in figures 4.3, 4.4 and 4.5, the students needed to think about how to build the tallest possible free-standing structure using only toothpicks and Play-Doh. The first part of the activity entailed individual journal writing. Students wrote and drew plans for the structures.

FIGURE 4.3 Engineering Challenge with Toothpicks and Play-Doh

In the next phase, students met with their tablemates to share and discuss ideas. Caren called out the Levels of Listening and other SEL skills they had been taught. In this way, the opportunities for RI and stronger ties were built into the lesson.

Students were extremely engaged in all aspects of the activity and came up with some brilliant ideas for building strong, tall structures. The lesson entailed physics, geometry, data, and English language development. This type of content integration provides multiple access points for students and also maximizes use of time. Rather than feeling pressured to teach each subject separately and sequentially each day, teachers can incorporate multiple subjects at the same time. The opportunities for friendship connections and communication are baked into the structure. By providing an engaging task and scaffolding the group work, teachers build students' interpersonal skills and relational connections.

FIGURE 4.4 Engineering Challenge Teamwork

FIGURE 4.5 Engineering Challenge Collaborative Implementation of Ideas

Caren's debrief of the lesson included content questions:

"What did you learn?"
"Did you notice anything about the structures that worked well?"
"What shapes seemed especially strong?"
"Why do you think that is true?"

She also took a few minutes to focus on the social aspects:

"What went well with your group?"
"What was challenging with your group?"
"How did you decide what type of tower to build?"
"What advice would you give to other students who are going to try this challenge?"

Students were honest and reflective in their responses:

"We all worked together, but some of us were not on the same page."

"The team voted!"

"Make a plan B!"

"We tried one idea and it didn't work, then we tried another idea and it worked a little better."

Integrating Friendship Reflections across the Curriculum

Taking the time to debrief and process activities and experiences yields extremely positive benefits. Students might work together on a group task but that doesn't mean they necessarily learned much about working together. They need time to reflect on how it went, what factors contributed to the results, and how they impacted the group. Some of this reflection occurs during morning meetings and community circles, but it can happen more often and in other parts of the day.

Every day, across the curriculum opportunities to strengthen friendship ties exist. We encourage teachers to identify at least one lesson a day in which the students work together and then reflect on what went well and what was challenging. Start with a 5-minute interactive warm up game, then do a quick (10 minutes or less) intro for the activity. Allot most of the time for students to work together on an interesting and engaging task (solving a math puzzle, analyzing a fictional character's motivations and making predictions, creating a timeline or graphic organizer to explain a historical event, doing a STEAM challenge, creating a poster or infographic to summarize a book or literary passage, etc.). Often having students work in pairs before working in larger groups helps scaffold skills that lead to effective collaboration. Do a 5-minute debrief about the social aspects of the work.

"What went well when you were working together?"

"What was challenging?"

"What's something helpful that your partner did?"

"What did you contribute to your group's efforts?"

"Would you like to compliment someone who was especially helpful?"

The lessons chosen for these SEL debriefs need to have a lot of space for students to come up with their own ideas and authentically grapple with an open-ended problem. If the activity is too structured, students don't have as many chances to talk and think together. We don't expect teachers to develop new curriculum. Using an activity from a textbook or other resource works well as long as there's an authentic reason for students to talk and work together.

In one meeting we had with teachers, the question of classroom structures arose. We asked about specific structures teachers can use to build friendships in their classrooms. After talking in small groups, the teachers generated the following list:

1. Randomize groups in different ways so that different groups work together—sometimes heterogeneously, sometimes based on skills or interest.
2. Regularly use community circles and community games.
3. Organize activities so they encourage group work.
4. Create systems and protocols to help students navigate friendships (e.g., sentence frames, strategic pairings, or groupings).
5. Model situations with the students so they can see effective communication and connections (healthy friendships).
6. Explicitly teach about empathy and kindness (connect to friendships).
7. Address teasing/spreading rumors.
8. Do morning meeting activities and games.
9. Use daily situations as contexts.
10. Distribute students into different groups when doing different activities.
11. Refer to everyone in the classroom as friends.
12. Positive vibes only—model and insist on positive language and prosocial behaviors.
13. Randomize grouping and show you expect everyone to work with everyone.
14. Ask questions and debrief friendship connections across content areas.

Many of these ideas and structures can be implemented multiple times each day. Teachers who consciously plan for building friendship ties and use the survey maps to dig into friendship networks in their classrooms can profoundly impact their students' experiences and relationships with each other.

Considering the Physical Environment

Most classroom teachers have enormous latitude in how they set up their classrooms. The constraints of space and furniture impact the options but many possibilities exist. In addition to furniture placement, seating assignments usually fall to teachers' discretion. While not often highlighted or discussed, these factors can play a huge role in how students interact with each other. As Christoforos Mamas points out, "Proximity is a way to build friendship."

The survey data from the SNA Toolkit can inform teachers' thinking about their classrooms as physical environments. Kim, a fifth-grade teacher, used her class's friendship map to help her think about seating. She added the question, "Whom would you like to know better?" on her students' surveys so she could see where new friendship connections could be fostered. She put students who nominated each other at the same table. This allowed her to use the survey for action-research. She could administer the survey again and see if the student's friendship ties had changed or strengthened after the seating intervention.

Many teachers have their students sit in groups and give them work to do together. Sometimes a simple impediment like desk size or arrangement can get in the way.

Although Figure 4.6 looks like a table where six students can work together, actually only four students at a time can interact.

1	3	5
2	4	6

FIGURE 4.6 Table Arrangement

Students 1 and 2 are significantly distanced and blocked from Students 5 and 6, so it's unlikely that they'll talk even though they're all at the same table. Having fewer desks pushed together can give the students more opportunities to interact meaningfully. Figure 4.7 shows an alternative table arrangement that gives students more access to each other.

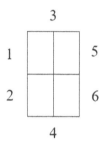

FIGURE 4.7 Alternative Table Arrangement

Often teachers cluster multilingual students together so they can support each other in their home language as needed. This proximity, along with the shared language, fosters strong friendship ties. It might also isolate the students from other classmates, so flexibility in space and grouping plays an important role in classroom social dynamics. One local teacher decided to do away with desks and set up her classroom "like a Starbucks." She wanted her students to have choice in where they might work and who they might sit near. She also wanted to give her students different types of seating (and standing) options. We encourage teachers to literally "create space" for students to interact and connect in various settings.

Beyond the Classroom: Schoolwide Structures to Promote Relational Inclusivity

Inarguably, teachers have tremendous influence over what goes on in their classrooms. They can have a huge impact on the routines, tone, space, and connections within their classroom community. Using the SNA Toolkit, they can deliberately structure activities and the classroom itself to promote SEL skills and expand/deepen friendship ties. However, the classroom is situated within a school and there are also schoolwide factors and structures that can help or hinder friendship ties.

Schedules, lunch protocols, recess structures, dismissal routines, and more affect ways students can connect with each other. Often these schoolwide structures have an especially profound impact on SPED students. If SPED students have different recess schedules and eat lunch separately or at a separate table, they miss out on chances to connect with their general education peers. Conversely, general education students need to connect across a diverse spectrum and learn the skills and empathy required to develop strong friendship ties.

Some intentional schoolwide structures require little ongoing maintenance and can have huge impacts on student connections. For example, to build connections between SPED and general education students, Baker Elementary assigns general education "buddies" who greet each SPED student in the morning and walk them to their classroom. These welcoming gestures and the direct connections between students who don't typically interact create schoolwide feelings of inclusion.

SPED students are often mainstreamed for parts of the school day. Some of the mainstreaming parameters revolve around student need, subject matter, class schedules, and IEPs. The mainstreaming protocol can also involve the students. The SPED teacher might visit the general education classroom to give students some background and strategies for connecting with their SPED classmates. General education students could also visit the SPED classrooms to get a sense of the types of work and support offered to their SPED peers.

Relational inclusivity may happen more easily in non-academic moments. Lunch, recess, library time, enrichment classes, extra-curricular clubs are all excellent forums for developing friendships and learning to use SEL skills. These non-academic arenas allow students' ideas and talents to shine. Intentionally including students and dedicating some time to reflecting on social dynamics can turn these non-academic, schoolwide structures into SEL goldmines. A thoughtful school administrator, working with a few teacher leaders, can make a few minor adjustments that could have a profound effect on relational inclusivity and schoolwide friendship ties.

Some schools we worked with also had student-led conferences as an annual forum for students to share their growth and goals with their families and community members. Asking students to include a slide about their SEL strengths and/or their friendship goals can lead to further discussion and awareness. It also conveys the message that these components have high value.

Summary

Research tells us that friendships in school matter—both socio-emotionally and academically. Teachers and school leaders have the ability to support friendship ties at the individual, classroom, and schoolwide levels. We encourage educators to use the SNA survey and maps to learn more about existing friendship ties, and then consider some of the suggestions in this chapter to make friendship and Relational Inclusivity an explicit goal.

Notes

1. Find The Responsive Classroom at https://www.responsive-classroom.org.
2. Learn more about Restorative Justice at https://www.iirp.edu/news/time-to-think-using-restorative-questions.
3. Find the CASEL Framework at https://casel.org/fundamentals-of-sel/what-is-the-casel-framework/.
4. Learn more about the 5 Levels of Listening at https://www.forbes.com/sites/forbescoachescouncil/2020/02/04/the-sixth-commandment-of-highly-effective-leadership-be-an-effective-listener/?sh=5a46feff7291.
5. Find this resource at https://reachingexceptionallearners.com/prompting-hierarchy-in-special-education/.

5

Whom Do You Play with at Recess?

What the Research Tells Us

♦ Play promotes students' sense of self-worth and their confidence.
♦ Play provides students with opportunities to solve complex problems, experiment, and gain knowledge about their own character.
♦ Play promotes creativity, cooperation, and adaptability.

Play has been shown to directly support the development of children's social skills, like empathy and self-regulation, and indirectly impact academic and social learning (Hirsh-Pasek et al., 2009). Outdoor play has been shown to promote positive physical health, including building children's bone density and immune systems (Dyment et al., 2009), enhancing students' confidence and self-esteem (Ginsberg et al., 2007), and promoting their cognitive and emotional well-being (Bento et al., 2017). Outdoor play inspires creativity, experimentation, cooperation, and creative thinking in children of all ages (Bento et al., 2017). Children who engage in outdoor play are able to interact with unpredictable, constantly changing natural environments in loud, boisterous gross motor activities, and to

DOI: 10.4324/9781003398738-5

experience a sense of freedom that classroom activities may not allow. Research shows that 170 million school children are overweight (Lobstein et al., 2004), and physical activity potentially mitigates this growing health concern for our nation's children (CDC, 2011).

Historically, U.S. schools have provided regularly scheduled recess periods for all elementary school students (Slater et al., 2012). Recess is an ideal place for students to let off steam and engage in physical activity. Children who participate in consistent recess activities during the school day have more positive mental health outcomes—less depression, lower anxiety, and increased confidence (Ahn et al., 2011; Erwin et al., 2013). Consistent recess activity at school has also been shown to promote more appropriate classroom behaviors and more sustained attention in the classroom (Barros et al., 2009; Pellegrini et al., 1995). Play during recess is a powerful learning tool for children of all ages. Understanding the relational aspects of children's play in school can be an important tool for teachers to leverage to further promote both social and cognitive outcomes for their students.

Survey/Map Examples

As the research shows, the potential benefits of play and recess are numerous. The importance of play cannot be discounted and students rarely have time for free play in classrooms because of the pressures standardized tests place on many teachers and administrators. The SNA Recess survey question provides information that can be particularly valuable to classroom teachers. Typically, classroom teachers are not with their students during recess, so they don't have firsthand knowledge of how children are playing, including who is or is not playing together. Yet, many teachers often receive the "collateral damage" of difficult or hostile recess interactions. Students may return to class upset, feeling angry, bullied, or lonely. The SNA recess survey maps can help teachers get a sense of who is spending time with whom and who is disconnected.

The recess map is usually less dense than the friendship map, but more dense than the help and talk maps. Many same grade classrooms attend recess at the same time so students have more recess playmates than just their classroom peers. Often students have siblings, neighbors, teammates, or friends outside of their classroom whom they spend time with at recess. These connections don't show up on the classroom-only surveys. Certainly there are overlaps between friendships and spending time at recess together. Anita explained the difference between a good friend and a very good friend in terms of recess. "I mean, a great friend would be there with you at recess and wherever you go. And a good friend would be with you but sometimes leave."

Figure 5.1 shows a recess map from a fifth-grade classroom. The teacher can see that most of the students have at least a few connections to other classmates during recess. However, Students 2 and 14, both SPED students, have no nominations. (They didn't take the survey so they didn't have the opportunity to nominate anyone). However, Student 20, also a SPED student, seems fairly well integrated into the recess network. A follow-up action might be to explore the mechanisms that support Student 20 and consider how they might be applied to Students 2 and 14.

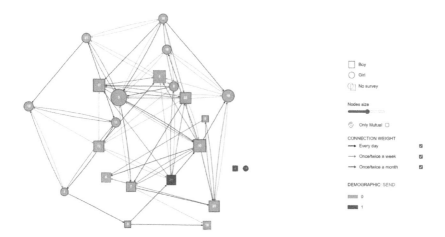

FIGURE 5.1 Recess Network Map by SPED Status

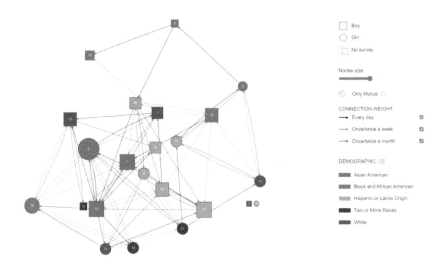

FIGURE 5.2 Recess Network Map by Race/Ethnicity

Figure 5.2 shows the same classroom's map but with a focus on race and ethnicity. The teacher can see that several students are highly connected to their classmates across demographic characteristics. These students might be considered "influencers," so supporting these individuals in their social and play skills might have significant ripple effects on the rest of the class. Again there are a few students with no connections. The teacher might invest time in understanding what these "outlier" students are doing at recess, perhaps taking a few minutes to go out to recess one day to observe and document the recess activities of the isolated students. The teacher might also ask the recess supervisors or college volunteers to keep an eye on the student and report back. What activities are occupying their time during recess? Are they playing near certain kids? Are there certain kids that invite the isolated child to play? Could those kids be paired up during classroom activities so they can extend their play into recess?

Some students may have a more elevated "social status" at recess than they do in the classroom. This information is very valuable to teachers as they can build on the strengths students have outside of the classroom to increase connectedness and positive interactions within the classroom. For example, Nilu noticed that one of her students, Roland, had many more recess nominations than friendship nominations, which is not typically the case for most students. Nilu wondered why some of Roland's classmates chose to play with him at recess but then didn't choose him as a friend in the classroom.

Another issue that many of our teacher collaborators described was chronic absenteeism—when a student is absent from school at least 10% or more of their allotted school days (CA Dept of Education, 2023). Many students who do not consistently attend school may be challenged to make meaningful connections at recess. When Christian looked at his third graders' recess surveys, he noticed that one of his students had very few nominations. He hypothesized that this student's chronic absenteeism precluded them from making robust connections during recess.

Learning from the Students

Talking to students while they take the survey yields valuable insights. Caren sat with a fourth grader while they were answering the question: "Whom do you play with at recess." The student did not nominate any classmates and explained, "I don't play with anyone at recess. I sit and talk to a fifth grader." Caren asked how the student felt about that and the student replied, "Fine." So, what might have looked like an issue on the survey map—a student who didn't play with any classmates at recess—turned out to be a non-issue. Checking in with students before making assumptions can save a lot of time and energy. In future iterations of survey questions related to recess, the survey could be expanded to include the names of children in other classrooms who have recess at the same time (e.g., all the children in one grade).

Having short conversations (small group or whole class) also reveals a lot about students' recess experiences. Susan asked her sixth graders why students needed recess. One student explained, "I think recess is important because some kids can't really sit through the whole lesson. And I think you should have a time where our minds should take a rest and focus on our friends and talking more."

Another student passionately articulated why teachers need to know what's going on during recess:

> It's just that there's a lot of drama going around in school. And I think because no one knows. And not even the teachers…there's drama and people being mean to you, people swearing at each other, people spreading rumors about each other, people lying to each other, and it's something that I've been wanting to get off my chest because it's kind of weird because I'm surprised that none of the teachers—the teachers think that we're just innocent students, perfect, just a normal life, and then in reality it's just people being mean to each other, spreading rumors and people not respecting each other and treating each other badly and it's just so annoying.

By bringing students' awareness to the value of recess, students have more understanding of their roles and reasons for positive interactions with their peers. Furthermore, when teachers have a greater sense of the connections and interactions happening during recess, they might be able to better leverage the strengths in their classroom and address SEL issues more expeditiously.

Explicit Instruction in Prosocial and Positive SEL Skills

In some ways, recess is a proving ground. Teachers spend a great deal of time and energy fostering a positive classroom community and helping students with their SEL skills. But does it transfer to recess when students have more freedom and less supervision? How can teachers help students bridge classroom skills and expectations to the recess environment? We know that bullying, inappropriate language, and unsafe behaviors are more likely to occur at recess than in the classroom. Certainly teachers cannot take on the responsibility of everything that goes on during recess but they can try to equip their students to be more confident and compassionate in general.

Nilu and Adele noticed that many of their students lacked confidence and positive attitudes about themselves, which translated to negative behaviors and interactions in and out of the classroom. Adele explained, "It's hard for students to be confident, love themselves." To address the issue, they devised a homework assignment.

We had them reflect on the things that they loved about themselves. We had them ask one person from home what do you love about me? Have a teacher or school person write what they love about them. They have evidence of why these people love them and why they should love themselves. It's an important step before they can be confident about themselves.

Nilu added that they deliberately included a question about why their teachers love them. "My teacher loves me because… You need to ask me. You have to ask them. It's really important that you hear it. It's kind of a vulnerable posture to ask someone that." Many students reported that they didn't know why their teachers loved them. Love is not typically a focus in school. But perhaps if students felt loved at school, they would feel more confidence and joy. Bringing such confidence and joy to recess opens possibilities for more social interaction and further connections.

Facilitating Activities That Maximize Engagement and Collaboration

This part is tricky. Teachers usually aren't at recess with their students so they can't directly facilitate activities. They can do some quick pre- and post-recess activities that might help students focus on positive engagement and practice SEL skills. Asking students to write in their journals, write a sentence on an exit slip, or just turn and talk to a partner can facilitate more self-awareness and encourage more collaborative play at recess.

TABLE 5.1 Recess Time Prompts

Situation	Teacher Questions
Right before students go outside to recess:	• What is your goal for recess today? • How can you be a good friend at recess? • What are you going to pay attention to at recess? • What's one new thing you might try at recess? • Whom could you invite to join you today? • How might you handle a challenging recess situation?
When students return from recess:	• Did you achieve your recess goal? • What did you do to be a good friend at recess? • What did you notice at recess? • What new or different thing did you do at recess? • Whom did you include at recess? • Who was a good friend to you today? What did they do?

Table 5.1 has a few quick prompts teachers might use to help their students focus on SEL and connections at recess time. We recommend choosing one question at a time and revisiting some of the questions over the course of the year to build relational inclusion.

Some teachers do quick (5–10 minute) community circles after lunch or recess. These circles give students a chance to transition back to classroom norms. The circles also help students process their recess experiences and reflect on recess events and interactions. Teachers can ask students if they saw or heard anything wonderful at recess. They can also ask if any student has a compliment or thank you for a friend. One teacher that we've worked with described an activity that allowed for students to reflect and process the social dynamics of recess. Every day after recess she gathered her kindergartners on the carpet and introduced the activity: "Toodles and Spleen." "Toodles" is an observation of kind/respectful behavior. Spleen is an observation of a bad behavior (hitting or pushing). The teacher asked the kids to talk about what Toodles and Spleens they observed on the playground. If a student noticed a "spleen," they would talk about what happened and how to resolve the problem. The teacher and the student who did the problem behavior would then follow up with the individual student to make sure they felt seen and heard. This was an opportunity to address unresolved problems (hitting, pushing). And also a time to reinforce the helpful, kind, or respectful behaviors.

Our colleague, Kathrina, uses a "Triple A" protocol to structure quick debriefs with her students. She asks if anyone has an Appreciation, Aha Moment, or Apology they would like to share. This quick prompt can apply to almost any experience. It works especially well as a transition activity when students return to the classroom from recess, highlighting connections and SEL skills.

Journal writing is another impactful way for students to transition back into the classroom and reflect on their recess experiences. Any of the suggested discussion prompts could also serve as quickwrites or journal prompts.

Considering the Physical Environment

Schools vary vastly in spaces and structures for recess. At some sites, there are designated spaces for activities and grade levels. At other sites, the playground is open to all students. Some schools emphasize the physical opportunities recess affords, while others allow students to sit and visit.

Baker Elementary has designated spaces on the playground that encourage specific types of activities. In addition to sports areas—soccer field, running track, basketball courts—Baker has a garden area where students can visit in the shade or tend to plants. Within the garden there is an area for drum circles led by trained fifth-grade leaders.

Features such as a garden, an art zone, a board game area, or a "buddy bench" encourage students to connect with each other in a peaceful, intentional manner. In addition to the physical space, designating student facilitators, volunteers, or paraprofessionals to lead activities like drum circles, restorative circles, or games provides structure for the activities and also develops leadership skills.

Beyond the Classroom: Bigger Picture Structures

In the high stakes testing environment, it's easy to overlook the value of play. As Peter Gray notes, "Creativity blossoms in play." Surely, educators recognize the importance of creativity both for intellectual development and personal satisfaction. Recess is the one designated time in the school day for play. Students benefit when schools understand the importance of what goes on at recess, rather than just treating it as a break. Gray explains why playing at recess has many SEL and relational inclusivity benefits as well:

> The reason why play is such a powerful way to impart social skills is that it is voluntary. Players are always free to quit, and if they are unhappy they will quit. Every player knows that, and so the goal, for every player who wants to keep the game going, is to satisfy his or her own needs and desires while also satisfying those of the other players, so they don't quit. Social play involves lots of negotiation and compromise.

We encourage school leaders to work with school staff to maximize the recess possibilities. Several questions can be structured to facilitate staff discussions about recess and RI.

1. Who is together at recess?
    Typically recess occurs by age and grade level. Many times the mainstreamed SPED students are not with their peers during recess. Thinking about schedules that allow SPED students to be with their general education peers during non-academic times is a powerful way to strengthen connections and appreciate the skills

and talents of all of the students. Another consideration is cross-age activities. Having older students work with younger students during recess gives them both leadership skills and a sense of belonging at school. The younger students benefit from older buddies who serve as role models and guides.

2. What interventions are available during recess?

Paraprofessionals usually do the heavy lifting at recess. While teachers are preparing and taking a short break, the paraprofessionals oversee recess time. In some schools the paraprofessionals are trained to lead specific activities rather than merely oversee the general situation. At Baker Elementary the school support staff, such as counselors and college volunteers, have responsibilities during recess. They lead groups and facilitate community circles and SEL based activities. They also coordinate "walking clubs" where students can simultaneously get physical exercise and have small group discussions.

3. What spaces exist for intentional connection?

The physical layout of the playground and other outdoor areas extend rich opportunities for connection. Games and sports such as soccer, basketball, and tetherball have clearly defined areas. Additionally, spaces such as gardens, friendship benches, and arts areas invite students to participate in activities that facilitate interaction and stronger ties over time.

4. What choices are offered to students?

The unstructured freedom of recess can give students important practice in planning and making choices. Not only can they choose what to do and whom to do it with, they can also set goals and monitor their progress. The adults at recess, equipped with some helpful questions, can casually ask students during recess, "How are you feeling?" "What are you going to do today?" "Which friends do you want to connect with?" "What are your hopes and dreams for recess today?" "Where do you want to spend your time today?"

These questions are particularly helpful when SPED students are included at recess with general education students. Asking both groups to intentionally make and state their choices gives the adults insights into who would like to play with whom and how they might make it happen.

Summary

Recess offers a fertile ground for students to practice the SEL skills that build Relational Inclusivity. Schools that appreciate the immense potential of recess implement deliberate structures to support students in their important recess work (play).

6

Whom Do You Go to for Help with Your Classwork?

What the Research Tells Us

- ♦ Peer academic support promotes positive psychological outcomes for students.
- ♦ Peer academic support enhances students' sense of belonging to school and improves academic performance.
- ♦ For historically marginalized students, peer academic support may buffer the opportunity gaps that exist in the education system.

Research shows that peer academic support is a valuable tool for students to succeed in school and in their social emotional development. Peer academic support has been shown to improve students' confidence, social skills, and their academic engagement (Brock & Huber, 2017; Scheef & Buyserie, 2020). Students who report more peer academic support have also reported having a stronger sense of belonging to school along with improved academic performance (Vargas-Madriz & Honishi, 2021). Students who also reported receiving peer academic support have also been shown to have expanded social networks and an increased number of friendship ties as compared to those that do not receive peer academic support (Carter et al., 2016). Carter and colleagues have also shown that peer academic

DOI: 10.4324/9781003398738-6

support enhanced students' understanding of their own academic development and the value that neurodiverse individuals have on academic development and self-advocacy in school.

Some studies show that peer academic support can be used to mitigate opportunity gaps that exist systematically across the education system. For example, some studies show that students who come from marginalized backgrounds and who use both formal and informal peer academic support programs are more academically successful and those students have more social connections in college (Tucker et al., 2020).

Survey/Map Examples

Classrooms with a robust network of peer academic support have significant advantages for both the students and the teacher. If everyone in the classroom is a learner AND a teacher, the opportunities for academic growth and achievement multiply exponentially. Teachers have a great deal of control over how they structure lessons and their classroom to maximize opportunities for students to work together and help each other.

Figure 6.1 shows the "help network" in a fifth-grade classroom. Except for Student 2, all the students have at least a few help connections. Who is Student 2 and what can be done to integrate them into the class's help network? Students 5, 16, 19, and 20 received many nominations from their classmates. Why are these particular students viewed as reliable helpers? What characteristics contribute to this perception among their classmates? And how can the classroom teacher leverage and highlight these students' skills so that others in the class can also be seen as equally skilled and helpful? The survey map prompts these types of questions and encourages teachers to do some informal action research to find answers.

Figure 6.2 reveals the same help network in terms of race/ethnicity. Here again we see a robust network of students with various connections. Some students have many nominations, and there's one outlier, Student 2, with zero connections. Questions immediately emerge from looking at this map. A closer look shows

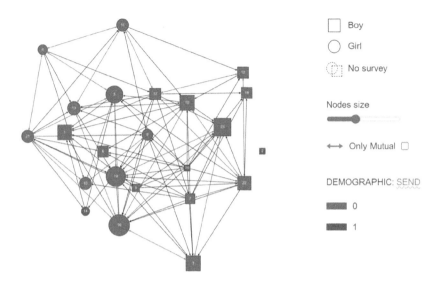

FIGURE 6.1 Help Network Map by SPED Status

that the students who received many nominations did not recip-rocate the nominations with classmates. What might that say? Is there a perceived hierarchy in the classroom with only a handful of students considered "smart" and worthy of helping others? If so, how can the perception be more widely distributed so that all students value the skills and intelligence of their classmates?

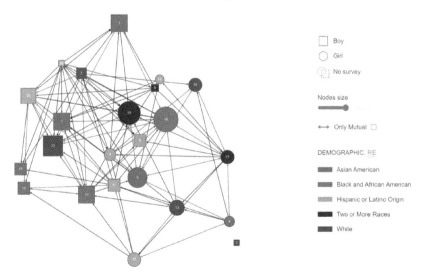

FIGURE 6.2 Help Network Map by Race/Ethnicity

When Natalie looked at her third- and fourth-grade students' Help Survey Maps, she had similar questions about her students' perceptions of varying academic abilities in the classroom. She noticed that her two highest performing students only nominated each other for help. Even high performing students benefit from more options, connections, and exposure to different learning styles. Not only do these connections increase the opportunities for collaboration and learning, they also strengthen the classroom's social network/RI as a whole.

Nilu noticed that one of her classroom practices might too heavily influence whom the students nominated for help. Nilu had assigned some of her students "TA" roles so that she would be interrupted less during small group instruction. This innovative practice both freed Nilu for more effective instruction and gave students within the classroom leadership roles. However, when completing the help survey, the designated "TAs" had much larger nodes than the rest of the students. Nilu realized that the "TA" status might have precluded students from considering non-TAs as potential helpers. By rotating the TA roles and making the opportunities for helping more widely and explicitly available, Nilu hoped to increase the help connections in her classroom. Nilu might also consider designating different kids as "TAs" during different learning activities. For example, certain kids who have grasped a math concept could be the TAs during the independent math activity and other students who have excelled in their essays could be considered TAs during the language arts independent activity.

Christian noticed a similar trend with his third graders. He had some "Bobcat Helpers" who wore special name tags and had a helping role during small group instruction and independent work time. The Bobcat Helpers had many nominations, while several of the other students in the class were relative outliers. Christian wondered if he could teach these outliers some specific games and activities to lead and make them Bobcat Helpers during certain times of the day. This adaptation might broaden the students' ideas about who can be helpful for certain types of learning activities.

Learning from the Students

Talking to students about helping and working together provides many insights about how individualized academic peer support can support student learning. Teachers can find out if students value the help of their friends and classmates. When asked if she preferred working alone or with friends one student replied:

> with friends because maybe if you're having a hard time—like on math or something—you can ask them, but not telling you the answer… And maybe you can solve the answer, and if you don't get it, well, you may ask the teacher.

The reasons why students value their classmates' help vary quite a bit. Alexia explained that she only goes to one student for help, "Just Harper—she helps me and she helps me get it right." Danielle had a different perspective. She was less concerned about getting her work right and more focused on friendship. She stated that her help network consisted of "Only Hattie. Even if she doesn't know, she tries to help me, she's a good friend." Gregorio had a very pragmatic approach to his help nominations. As he scanned the survey for names, he explained that he chose classmates who "help me a lot if I don't take notes."

Explicit Instruction in Prosocial and Positive SEL Skills

Classroom teachers have an important opportunity to impact the Help Networks in their classrooms. First, teachers influence the perceived academic status of their students. If a competitive, hierarchical structure exists, all students know who is a high achiever ("smart") and who is a low achiever ("not smart"). If a more communal, collaborative, and strengths-based approach is employed, students get the message that everyone is capable and everyone's ideas and contributions are valuable. The latter approach sets the stage for a robust help network. Beyond explicit messaging from the teacher, there are many other activities and structures that support academic peer support in the classroom.

Teachers who value partner and group work intentionally give their students a variety of experiences working together and helping each other. Starting with short, low cognitive load tasks helps scaffold group work and allows teachers to build on successes. Pairing students up for quick "turn and talks" is a great place to start. Initially, the prompts can be very engaging and topical, then prompts can gradually ramp up the academic focus until students are comfortable talking to each other and helping each other across the curriculum. Table 6.1 lists a few suggested partner prompts to scaffold students' academic dialogues.

The social dynamics when students help each other need to be acknowledged explicitly. Many teachers assign random groupings, seatings, and partnerships to convey the message that everyone is capable of working with everyone else in the classroom. These random assignments may lead to disappointment and frustration among students who were hoping to work with their friends. Addressing the issue directly is very effective. Telling students that in jobs and in real life, people work together and they will not always work with their friends. It is important

TABLE 6.1 Help Network Prompts

Type of Prompt	Sample Prompts
Early Partner Prompts (to build peer rapport)	What's your favorite thing in the classroom? Where would you like to spend more time in the classroom? Do you prefer to write with a pencil or pen?
Intermediate Academic Partner Prompts	What's one thing you're good at? What would you like to learn more about? Do you learn better by seeing, by hearing, or a different way?
Advanced Academic Partner Prompts	What is your answer to the problem? How did you get it? Listen to your partner's ideas and say the ideas back in your own words. Tell what's the same and different about your ideas/answers.

to learn how to work with people who are not your friends as long as you both understand what the job is and how to work together in a kind, respectful way. Also, when you work with different kinds of people you learn more.

In addition to random groupings for class work, many teachers also use strategic partners and groupings for different activities. When Kim looked at her fifth graders' survey results, she saw that quite a few students wished they knew other students better (an additional question she and her colleagues added to the SNA survey). With this information in mind, Kim reassigned table groups to give students who weren't friends a chance to get to know each other and work together. This type of "social engineering" combined with explicit guidance in collaboration broadens the connections within the classroom.

Often the SPED students are outliers in the help networks. This may be due in part to their schedules and availability, but it may also reflect deficit ideas and assumptions about the student's capabilities. Mary teaches a moderate-severe SPED class and had many suggestions for integrating the SPED students into the general education classroom's help networks. She suggested focusing on some of the life skill activities that the SPED students practice both in the SPED and general education classrooms. Subjects like cooking, time, measurement, and money might be opportunities for the SPED students to more fully participate and perhaps even co-lead a game or activity.

In order to break some of the deficit perspectives, Mary also suggested focusing on some of the skills and interests of the SPED students. For example, Mary had one student who was highly interested and competent in languages. This student could teach the rest of the class some words in different languages. Another student was a skilled artist who could do wonderful drawings for group projects. To further display the SPED students' abilities rather than "disabilities," Mary advocated for structured class time where her students can share dance, songs, hand games, mirror games, and readers' theater performances with younger students. In Nilu's fourth-grade classroom, the mainstreamed SPED students are assigned class jobs and participate in classroom community meetings. This non-academic inclusion reinforces the notion that the SPED students are important and contributing members of the classroom. Students are more likely to seek and offer help to classmates who are fully integrated into the fabric of the classroom.

Facilitating Activities That Maximize Engagement and Collaboration

Perhaps one of the most effective ways to maximize helping engagement and collaboration comes with open-ended, problem-solving tasks. Let kids be brilliant and creative, let them guide the work and bring their own experiences in. By facilitating learning opportunities that have multiple solution pathways, teachers open the door for students' ideas and creativity. Rather than a more traditional focus on one right answer and speed, teachers can offer students activities that require thinking, com-munication, trial and error, and group effort. As students experi-ence more of these moments with different peers, they begin to see the value and potential help that their classmates bring to the table. An example of such an activity is "Tape Town" which we implemented with Christian, Cathy, and Natalie's third- and fourth-grade students when they visited our UCSD campus. While we don't advocate doing this activity with 70 students at once (it did work, though), we do think the success of the activity with such a large and diverse group indicates its potential for creating more help connections.

The primary objective of Tape Town is for students to build a town on a large piece of butcher paper using only markers, col-ored pencils, and masking tape.

Caren introduced the activity quickly so the students could get to work. First she asked students to think about all the things they might find in their town. As students shared, Christian recorded their ideas on chart paper. This chart would serve as a reference once the students got to work. Then Caren explained the goal and materials available. She had students do a quick partner talk to discuss how they might use the

FIGURE 6.3 Tape Town Activity

masking tape to build structures. The students came up with many great ideas—fold it, twist it, layer it, rip it, curl it, wrap it around something—which were all noted on another piece of chart paper. Caren concluded the intro by asking students what are some helpful ways they might work together to create their town. Here again the students had a plethora of great suggestions—listen, help each other, say kind words, work together, make a plan. These suggestions were written on a third chart.

After passing out the materials, the students got to work. As shown in figures 6.3 and 6.4, students had to first draw the Tape Town and then use the tape to make the buildings 3D. There were some challenges at the beginning. Masking tape is not a typical building material, so the students had to practice different techniques and decide what worked based on the item they wanted to create. The teachers circulated as the students worked. Their primary role was to ask questions and help students pay attention to each other and work together. As the students became more comfortable using the materials, they began to talk in depth about what they wanted to include in their town, where they wanted to put it on the butcher paper, and how they might create it. The exchanges between students included

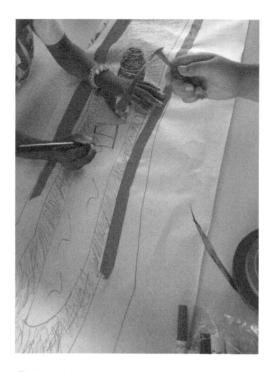

FIGURE 6.4 Tape Town Activity

many ideas and suggestions. The teachers emphasized the great ideas that were being generated and the wonderful ways students were helping each other and building on each other's ideas. Making the helping aspect of the work visible and explicit brings its value to the forefront.

The helping and collaboration happened partly by the nature of the task and partly because the teachers allowed the students to direct their own work and make their own decisions. The teachers also served as connectors, pointing out students' creativity and innovative use of the tape. They also helped students connect Tape Town to what they did and knew about in their own town. For example, one of the students was a paper boy and he began rolling the tape into "newspapers" that could be delivered to the buildings and homes other students created. Additionally, teachers assisted when conflict or disagreement arose. Caren noticed that one of the students accused another student of "copying" because they were both making stores. Caren pointed out "copying" meant someone recognized a good idea. The original student made a Walmart and the "copier" was making a Target. Caren talked with the students about how their structures were turning into a shopping area in Tape Town. Other students then started making more stores, and parking lots and created "The Tape Town Mall."

Integrating Helping Reflections Across the Curriculum

The Tape Town activity offered a natural opportunity to discuss the benefits of helping and working together. After the students had worked on their towns and had done a "gallery walk" to see others' work, they had a closing discussion about the experience. Caren first asked some general questions such as

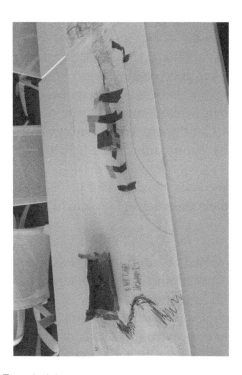

FIGURE 6.5 Tape Town Activity

"What did you like about this activity?" and "What did you learn?" Many students shared that they liked working together which provided a springboard for Caren to delve deeper. She structured a "think, pair, share" in which she first asked individual students to quietly think about things their group mates did that were helpful and what they did to help their group mates. Next, students shared their thoughts with a partner. After the partner talk, Caren led a brief whole-group discussion in which students shared their ideas about helping and helpful behaviors. She recorded the student-generated list of helpful behaviors on a chart for students to see.

Considering the Physical Environment

Here again, classroom teachers impact helping connections enormously. How the room is arranged, and most importantly, how seating is organized, controls who gets help, who gives help, and who works in isolation. Further, the seating arrangements give strong messages to students about who teachers believe are good/bad or high/low. Teachers use many criteria to determine seating arrangements in their classrooms. These criteria include student need, behavior, language, ability, strategic pairings, and more. We encourage teachers to consider how all these decisions impact the helping networks in their classrooms.

As teachers become more deliberate in the physical arrangement and seating in their classrooms, they might ask themselves these questions:

Are students seated at individual desks or in groups?
Are students in randomized groups, teacher assigned groups, or student chosen groups?
Are seating and grouping assignments flexible or rigid?
Do students have opportunities to choose whom they want to work with and where they want to work?
Do students have places where they can quietly work on their own as needed?

Do all students have opportunities to highlight their strengths and expertise?

Is everyone in the classroom space considered a teacher and a learner?

While there aren't necessarily "right answers" to these questions, teachers who have thought about these issues and take a deliberate, student-centered approach tend to create safe classroom communities in which helping networks can grow and strengthen.

Beyond the Classroom: Bigger Picture Structures

Since most academic work happens in the classroom, most peer academic support opportunities reside there as well. However, school leaders and teams of teachers can actively develop a culture of helping and peer support at the schoolwide level. Elementary school Director, Melissa, sees the helping maps data as an opportunity for teachers to solve problems in grade level teams. She plans to have teachers' teams explore questions such as "Whom are kids going to for help? Is there a certain type of kid? How can we leverage this information?" Not only will these questions inform some of the actions teachers take within their classrooms, they also make peer academic support a topic worthy of time and exploration.

Fifth-grade teacher Kim sees peer academic support as crucial for her students as they prepare to transition to middle school. She wants her students to learn the skills to support each other as the academic demands increase and she wants students to "pass on" this knowledge. Middle school students visit Kim's fifth graders in the spring to help demystify and prepare them for starting middle school in the fall. Kim wonders if her fifth graders could perform a similar service for fourth graders entering fifth grade. Can they prepare slides, pamphlets, and presentations to help the fourth graders succeed in fifth grade? And might these sorts of explicit helping traditions become a part of the school culture?

Summary

The benefits of having students help each other with their school-work cannot be overstated. Not only does it free the teacher for more direct, concentrated work with small groups and individuals, it allows the students themselves to improve academically and connect more strongly with their peers.

7

Whom Do You Talk to If You Are Having a Bad Day?

What the Research Tells Us

♦ Emotional well-being impacts students' mental and physical well-being.
♦ Friendships have been shown to buffer against the negative effects of bullying or other types of victimization that decreases a students' emotional well-being.

Negative emotional well-being in the form of peer victimization or loneliness is prevalent in schools, and it has significant mental and physical health effects for children and adolescents (Schacter, 2021; Zeedyk et al., 2016). Bullying is particularly prevalent in the lives of SPED students (Zeedyk et al., 2014). For all, peer emotional support in the form of friendships can buffer the effects of peer victimization or other negative emotional experiences that prompt students to report "having a bad day" (Boivin et al., 2010; Cuadros & Berger, 2016; van der Meulen et al., 2021). It can be difficult for some students, especially students with disabilities, to build social connections and develop their peer networks to support their individual emotional well-being given the ambiguous process of making friends. Previous studies have identified structured interventions to support students

DOI: 10.4324/9781003398738-7

with varying abilities to make peer connections during unstructured times at school (recess). For example, peer buddying, social lunch clubs, and peer networks have all been shown to support friendship development for these students (van der Meulen et al., 2021). As more students with disabilities are being included in general education settings (McLeskey et al., 2012), it is important for teachers to add tools to their pedagogical toolbox that support students to develop their reliable peer support network that could buffer the effects of negative emotional well-being.

Survey/Map Examples

Perhaps the most telling survey question revolves around the Bad Day. Here students confront their feelings of trust, vulnerability, and deep connection. Certainly there is overlap between very good friends and whom to talk to on a Bad Day. But there is also a sense of compassion and integrity that students seek in their classmates. The friend you have lunch with and play with at recess is not necessarily the person you trust with your secrets and sensitive feelings. Not surprisingly, the Bad Day networks are often the least dense. The nominations and connections are often non-mutual and the connections (and disconnections) between students become clearer. Having a more distributed network of emotional support can ease the burden for teachers who typically handle the bulk of students' emotional needs in the classroom. Teachers who know their emotionally trustworthy students can leverage their support to de-escalate issues and provide comfort to students having a Bad Day.

There are many reasons why students might be having a Bad Day—bullying, issues at home, poor sleep, a bad grade, an incarcerated family member, rocky friend relationships, illness, and more. While the surveys and maps don't dig into the various causes, they do illuminate which students are viewed as supportive allies. Figure 7.1 demonstrates the often thin and unbalanced connections in the Bad Day networks. Many of the students have fewer than three nominations. A few students, like Students 16, 19, and 23, have five or more nominations but they

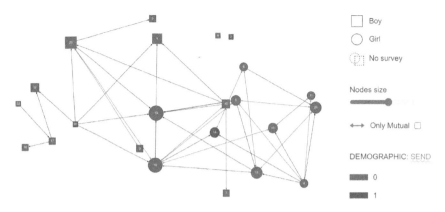

FIGURE 7.1 Bad Day Network Map by SPED Status

only nominated one or two of their classmates. Interestingly, most of the nominations are non-mutual. Many questions arise from this map. Are the mutual connections in the map considered by students to be very good friends? Why do some of the students have significantly more nominations? What's going on with the students who didn't nominate any of their classmates? Why do two students have no connections in either direction?

Figure 7.2 sparks similar questions. What are the attributes of Students 16 and 19 that give their classmates emotional trust in them?

Nilu was very interested in her fourth-graders' map. She noticed a lot of non-mutual connections. She also noticed one

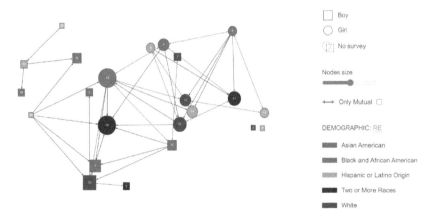

FIGURE 7.2 Bad Day Network Map by Race/Ethnicity

student who received a lot of nominations and hypothesized that, "A lot of people felt like they could talk to him. He's a more reserved kid, but he's very well-liked…He's never mean spirited. He's never been unkind to anyone." This prompted Nilu to think about "personality traits of kids that attract others." Christian also made some interesting observations about his third-graders' Bad Day map. He noticed immediately that all the outliers with no connections were SPED students. He also noticed that one of his students nominated 10 classmates but no one nominated him. Christian noted that this student seeks out and wants to talk to other students but lacks the skills. Christian was working with this student on some SEL goals and was eager to see how the map might change toward the end of the school year. Several teachers wondered how much physical presence factored into the results. In many classrooms the students with the fewest Bad Day connections were chronically absent students and/or students with disabilities who were included into general education classrooms for part of the day. Perhaps a certain level of familiarity is required for students to build trust and emotional connections.

Leah noticed that her fifth-graders' Bad Day nominations concentrated around students in the class who had positive social attributes and also tended to be more quiet. She wondered if she might find ways to bolster these students' status and visibility in the class. Similarly, Nilu noticed that some of the students who had many "friend" nominations did not have any "Bad Day" nominations. These students with significant friend nominations tended to be louder and more social, but not necessarily kind or empathetic. Nilu reflected on one "popular" student, "Everyone thinks he's the coolest or the best in class. But that's not someone who the others feel safe with."

Learning from the Students

Sitting with a fourth grader while she answered the Bad Day question quickly uncovered some important information. As Dorothea went through the list of names, she announced she was not picking Leilah because, "Leilah bullied me." Learning about this issue prompted an immediate discussion with Leilah and Dorothea to address the bullying.

Classroom meetings and small group discussions also bring important insights. A sense of mutual trust underlies students who nominate each other for the Bad Day question. As one sixth grader explained:

> Our friendship is great. If she falls, I help her. If I fall, she helps me. And if I'm having a Bad Day, she always tries to put a smile on my face. And ever since I came, she has always helped me and always been a great friend.

Trust again played a major role in seeking support for a bad day. When Christoforos interviewed a fifth grader he asked, "And so you have a bad day, do you prefer to talk to your close friends or to your teacher about it?" The student replied, "My close friends. Close friends and teacher, both of them. Because that's the only people I can trust."

Explicit Instruction in Prosocial and Positive SEL Skills

It's difficult to "teach trust," but there are sets of behaviors that make students more likely to be trusted. Teaching these behaviors and also helping students recognize these traits can expand and strengthen Bad Day networks. The survey maps give teachers deeper insight into the connections students feel toward each other. Combining that information with what teachers know from observation and spending time with students can provide a powerful way for teachers to intentionally structure both academic and social experiences. Some of this type of work is subtle. Making sure the quiet, kinder students have more attention and status in the classroom means more students have access to a "Bad Day" resource and a positive SEL role model. However, too much public praise and compliments may have unintended negative consequences for the students and their relationships. Quiet students tend not to like being singled out, and too much praise from the teacher may lead to resentment from other students. The work of elevating a student's status in the classroom is subtle but vital.

What does it take to expand and strengthen the Bad Day networks in a classroom? SEL skills come to mind immediately. Both the student having the bad day and the student whom they go to need to exhibit a repertoire of SEL behaviors. Students having a bad day need to recognize their feelings, communicate their feelings in an effective manner, and ask for what they need. The students they go to for support need to listen, express empathy and kindness, and respond to the needs. These skills and awareness develop slowly over time with support. Indeed, many adults struggle with this level of communication and interpersonal trust.

A complicating factor lies in the causes of a bad day. Students experience myriad challenges in and out of school, with peers, school personnel, and with family. A "Bad Day" is not just one thing. Teachers might start by asking students what causes a Bad Day for them. This prompt could be used for journal writing to keep things private or it could be part of a community circle. Having students recognize some of the influences in their lives helps them develop a sense of control and predictability. When the classroom community is safe for whole group discussions, it's very powerful for students to hear about some of the challenges and influences their peers face. These discussions foster empathy and also help students see that many of the challenges are shared. Fourth-grade teacher, Adele, also noted the importance of recognizing the different causes of bad days. She categorizes students' concerns into three types: need to be addressed and resolved immediately, need an acknowledgement before moving on, and need a follow up in the future. These categories might help teachers both recognize types of bad day issues and use protocols that most effectively tend to issues without unnecessarily disrupting instructional time.

Visual art and theater activities open doors for students to explore emotions and scenarios that might be difficult to address in a too direct or too abstract manner. Guided drawing activities can be particularly powerful. Below is a simple sequence:

1. Teacher gives a few examples of when they felt *a little sad or frustrated* (e.g., they broke their pencil point, they forgot to bring their water bottle to school, they found a hole in their favorite shirt). Write these examples on the board.
2. Teacher asks students if they can think of any other experiences that could be *a little sad or frustrating*. Add a few of the student generated examples to the list.
3. Give each student a drawing paper and some pencils, crayons, or markers.
4. Have students fold their papers in fourths.
5. Direct students as follows. Give them 2 to 3 minutes to complete each section quietly.

   In the first box draw a time you were *a little bit sad or frustrated*.

   In the next box draw some lines and shapes that show how you felt.

   In the third box write some words that describe how you felt.

   In the last box draw some things that helped you feel better.

6. Students can share their papers with a partner. Students listening to classmates can practice giving kind and supportive responses. Volunteers might also share with the whole class if they are comfortable. Students can practice active listening and kind words.

Having a tangible product to share gives students ownership and control of their feelings. They are also slightly removed from their bad day because they are talking about the paper, not just themselves. We recommend addressing relatively minor events to keep the focus on the protocol for reflecting and expressing rather than bringing up some potentially traumatic events.

Interactive modeling and fishbowl scenarios also give students concrete examples of how to navigate both their own bad days and offering support to classmates in distress. The morning meetings and community circles offer opportunities to "act out" scenarios. One student can act out the "bad day situation" and another student can act as the supportive friend. The rest of the class observes the interaction and gives positive feedback and comments when it's done. Revisiting the "Levels of Listening" (see chapter 4) may prove helpful in these activities. Teachers can also have a list of scenarios ready to go in a "Bad Day" jar and then randomly pick one. Some ideas include:

We ran out of my favorite cereal this morning.
I broke my shoe lace.
My little sister scratched my arm and it hurts.
I did my homework but I left it on the table at home.
I forgot to bring my permission slip for the field trip.
I wanted to play basketball at recess but I didn't get to.
I stepped in a puddle when I was walking my dog.
My friend is absent and we were going to play together after school.
My mom got mad at me because I forgot to take out the trash.
My older brother wouldn't let me play video games.
I think my goldfish is sick.
I had a hard time with a writing assignment.

Over time students might write some of their own bad day prompts on small slips of paper and add them to the Bad Day jar. We recommend having the students write their names on their contributions so teachers can address issues as needed.

Integrating Bad Day Reflections Across the Curriculum

Many teachers start their day with some sort of morning meeting or community circle. A quick check in about students' emotional states can be very helpful for a number of reasons. First, teachers learn about immediate issues or concerns. They also get a sense of the general mood of the class and can identify individual students who might need a little extra attention or follow up.

Some of the teachers we worked with use visuals to help students communicate about their feelings in the morning. They show four numbered photos of faces with different emotions and ask which one best describes the students' feelings. Students show their responses with the corresponding number of fingers. This non-verbal response allows students to communicate without being put on the spot. Teachers also use visuals such as weather emojis, colors, and number scales. Teachers can follow up with questions such as "What can you do for yourself when you're having a Bad Day?" "What can your friends do for you when you're having a Bad Day?" "What can you do for friends who are having a Bad Day?"

Another simple way to integrate more Bad Day reflections into the day is by doing a check in at the start of a partner or group activity. Teachers can ask their students to "Talk to a partner about how you are feeling and what you need from your partner to work well together." This type of prompt not only prepares students to help each other, it also builds empathy and teaches SEL strategies. Similarly, teachers might ask students to reflect at the end of an activity or project.

What were your challenges?
Did you get stuck or frustrated?
How did you deal with it?
How did your partner help you?

Again the connection between academic and social emotional learning is integral. Engaging, collaborative activities present a context for authentic communication. If students are doing rote, independent work they don't have a chance to reflect on or practice important SEL skills. Cross-curricular opportunities abound. The arts offer a natural entry point for both expressing feelings and responding to the work of others. Read Alouds and children's literature bring in characters who experience Bad Days and a multitude of remedies to address their problems. Using literature gives teachers tangible ways for students to talk about their own connections to the problems presented. Some excellent Read Alouds include:

When Sophie Gets Angry[1]
Angry Cookie[2]
The Sour Grape[3]
Even Superheroes Have Bad Days[4]
I Am Human[5]
Grumpy Monkey[6]

Goal setting activities and student-led conferences also give students a context for reflecting on how they handle their Bad Days and how they support their classmates who are having a Bad Day. Kim and Leah have their fifth-grade students articulate a friendship goal. Deion's goal was "don't make people mad at me when I'm mad." While a seemingly simple goal, Deion needs to both recognize his own Bad Day (being mad) and empathize with others to achieve it. This type of goal setting activity can be revisited and reflected upon throughout the school year. The students can adjust their goals as they reflect on their progress.

Considering the Physical Environment

Many teachers have a "Quiet Corner" or other safe spaces for students to use when they are upset or need some time alone. The very fact that such a space exists communicates important messages to students. First, they can recognize and self-regulate when they are troubled. Second, they have agency to take action and move themselves to a space that helps them with self-care. Third, other students can see when students are in the space and know that this classmate is having a Bad Day and may need some comfort or support.

A "mailbox" or other place to write and share feelings gives students the message that their feelings matter and they have a forum for reaching out. The mailbox can be placed in the "Quiet Corner" so students can reflect on their feelings and communicate in writing. Teachers who check their mailboxes at the beginning or end of each day have timely information about their students' Bad Day circumstances. Suggesting some "Bad Day" writing prompts for students helps them frame and communicate their feelings.

Today I feel _____ because _____.
I can help myself feel better by _____.
I can ask my friends to help by _____.
I want my teacher to know that _____.

In addition to designated spaces, some teachers offer physical objects that students can use to both comfort themselves and communicate to others that they are having a Bad Day. A stuffed animal or totem that students can bring to their seats serves as both a comfort and signal that they are seeking support from classmates and the teacher.

Beyond the Classroom: Bigger Picture Structures

Many schools have buddy benches which can be a visual and physical signal that a student is feeling lonely and/or needs some support. Gardens and art tables are also places students can seek a calming location and the support of others.

Walking clubs led by para educators, volunteers, or school counselors create a natural and healthy way for students to connect with peers under the guidance of a caring adult. These walking clubs can be very fluid in membership or they can be structured to specifically support a targeted group of students. Often the clubs meet during recess, lunch, or after school. The goal is to give students practice with communicating effectively. This communication includes talking about their feelings and actively listening to others empathetically. Having an adult participant/facilitator ensures that students are practicing appropriate, helpful communication skills.

Truly any aspect of the school community can be a support for students having a bad day. School Director, Melissa Han, believes the onus is on the entire school to teach and model empathy.

She believes classroom and community agreements are not stagnant exercises performed and posted at the beginning of the year. Melissa advocates for a continual revisiting of "class rules" or "community agreements" based on issues that arise throughout the school year. As students learn to express their feelings, address issues, reach out to students who have been hurt, and agree to adjust their behaviors to make the school a safer space, they also learn how to recognize and address Bad Days.

Summary

Schools are places of learning, and teachers are not therapists. The limits to addressing the causes and results of students' Bad Days are stark. However, within the confines of the classroom and school environments, many interventions can be implemented that offer scaffolding and structures for students to navigate their emotions and have some agency with their Bad Days. By helping students recognize their Bad Days and teaching students how to support each other's emotional well-being, the Bad Day networks will strengthen and deepen.

Notes

1 Find the *When Sophie Gets Angry* Read Aloud at https://www.amazon.com/Sophie-Angry-Really-Really-Scholastic-Bookshelf/dp/0439598451/ref=sr_1_1?crid=1ZNZV1X7VPG4U&keywords=when+sophie+gets+angry+-+really%2C+really+angry%22+by+molly+bang&qid=1699031767&sprefix=when+molly+gets%2Caps%2C254&sr=8-1,

2 Find the *Angry Cookie* Read Aloud at https://www.amazon.com/Angry-Cookie-Laura-Dockrill/dp/1536205443/ref=sr_1_1?crid=2APZ9MLZB0U4&keywords=angry+cookie&qid=1696545559&sprefix=angry+cookie%2Caps%2C121&sr=8-1,

3 Find *The Sour Grapes* Read Aloud at https://www.amazon.com/Sour-Grape-Food-Group/dp/0063045419/ref=sr_1_1?crid=1KONMIGB5K1SG&keywords=sour+grape&qid=1696545622&sprefix=sour+gra%2Caps%2C115&sr=8-1,

4 Find the *Even Superheroes Have Bad Days Read* Aloud at https://
www.amazon.com/Even-Superheroes-Have-Bad-Days/
dp/1454913940/ref=sr_1_1?crid=3I5HGTTDJSVAH&keywords=
even+superheroes+have+bad+days&qid=1696545699&sprefix=
even+super%2Caps%2C114&sr=8-1,

5 Find the *I Am Human* Read Aloud at https://www.amazon.
com/I-Am-Human-Book-Empathy/dp/1419731653/ref=sr_
1_1?crid=112L5XQQ9QXFY&keywords=i+am+human&qid=
1696545721&sprefix=i+am+human%2Caps%2C117&sr=8-1.

6 Find the *Grumpy Monkey* Read Aloud at https://www.amazon.
com/Grumpy-Monkey-Suzanne-Lang/dp/0553537865/ref=
sr_1_2?crid=1BCAXL9E7FYUF&keywords=grumpy+monkey&
qid=1696550303&sprefix=grumpy+monkey%2Caps%2C148&
sr=8-2.

8

Moving Forward

Within these pages, we have provided a solid scientific research base demonstrating that *Relational Inclusivity* (RI) supports both SEL and academic work. We have also provided the SNA Toolkit as a way to gather data about connections and RI within a classroom. But tools and research are only as helpful as the ways in which they are used. We hope all the professionals in the school community—teachers, administrators, para educators, counselors, student teachers, staff, volunteers—will work together to think, talk, analyze data, ask questions, reflect, and take action to facilitate strong ties among students. We don't want to add more to our colleagues' plates. We want to add a new perspective on what's already on the plate. Honor and focus on the SEL work that is already happening and make sure it stays a priority throughout the school year.

What do we hope our readers will "take away" from this book? We want readers to feel comfortable and curious about the SNA Toolkit, and we want them to take a crack at using the tool. We want readers to feel motivated to implement some of the suggestions and activities presented in the chapters. Most importantly, we want readers to understand that research on SEL and RI shows profound positive impacts on academic outcomes. At their best, schools are intellectual communities. Investing time in SEL and focusing on RI is not a distraction or a loss of valuable instructional time. In fact, the opposite is true. Students with a sense of well-being and belonging experience greater academic success. Spending time on SEL and RI throughout the school year not only

DOI: 10.4324/9781003398738-8

creates a community of engaged students, it also creates a *community of engaged learners*. And learning is what school is about—especially for underserved, marginalized, and disconnected students who often miss out on meaningful learning opportunities.

We hope readers understand that this work can happen in conjunction with academic goals, not in competition with them. The false dichotomy of either SEL or academics needs to be replaced with a focus on the SEL opportunities that already exist within every lesson across all content areas. The tendency in K–12 to chop and parse time into small, unrelated content chunks deserves serious questioning. Creating a series of unrelated lessons not only misses opportunities for cross curricular connection, it causes a need to "squeeze" all these little chunks into the already limited school day. Rather than think of SEL as another chunk that has no room in the already packed school day, think of SEL as an added layer to each lesson. Within this book we've offered many ways to add an SEL element to lessons with simple tweaks or quick (5 to 10 minutes) discussions or reflection questions. The practice of incorporating a brief SEL element to one or two lessons per day will have an enormous positive effect on RI over the course of a school year. Our work in schools has also highlighted the many transition times that occur each day—arriving at school, entering the room in the morning, going to and returning from recess, lunch time, transitions between lessons and activities, getting ready for dismissal at the end of the day. Each of these transition times also can be purposed for SEL and relational inclusivity by implementing simple practices such as asking a quick reflective question, playing a quick cooperative game, structuring a brief partner talk, assigning buddies, or asking students to set a short-term SEL goal.

Working extensively in schools with students, teachers, and school leaders we absolutely understand the pressures and competing demands of K–12 education. And we still encourage our readers to prioritize SEL and RI. Not only does RI enhance the learning in the classroom, it also enhances the quality of life for all involved. People exist as social beings who thrive in connection with each other. We want those vital human connections for all students and we want the same for our colleagues who do the vital and challenging work of educating our youth.

We know school staff meet regularly for meetings and professional development. Could 5–10 minutes of some meetings be devoted to SEL and RI? School Director Melissa Han sees opportunities to facilitate conversations with her teachers. She envisions asking them to look at SNA data in grade level or collaborating teams. She plans to focus on the stories behind the data and what the stories' implications might have for classroom/schoolwide practices. Kathleen Gallagher acknowledges that her role as a principal often involves "putting out fires," but she can imagine incorporating discussions about RI into IEP meetings—specifically asking whom the student is friends with, what SEL goals the student has, and how to connect the student with more friends. This practice can become a regular part of the IEP and "students of concern" meeting protocol.

Relational inclusivity at the school or system level includes opportunities for community members to talk with each other and collaborate on meaningful goals. School leaders and teachers can look for structures that already exist (staff meetings, recess, after school programs, lunch time, IEP meetings, etc.) and facilitate opportunities for communication and relationships between:

♦ SPED teachers and general education teachers
♦ High social status students and marginalized students
♦ SPED students and general education students
♦ Credentialed teachers and para educators
♦ SPED teachers and general education students
♦ Students at different grade levels
♦ Students with different home languages and backgrounds
♦ Students who share common interests/hobbies.

Over time this deliberate work can create a common language and common goals for schoolwide SEL and RI. This work is not easy and doesn't happen overnight. But with patience and intentionality the culture of a school can shift toward an increasing awareness of SEL and a greater valuing of RI. Again, the work does not need to be "one more thing" that no one really has time for. It can simply be a slight shift in practice and focus in the already existing structures of school life. We advocate here for slow and deliberate attention rather than major changes or "the next new program." Administer the SNA surveys. Let the data, the observations, the reflections, and the discussions drive the work. Educators can regularly ask:

What are we noticing?
What assumptions are we making?
What stories do the data tell?
What might be going on?
Who surprised us? Why?
What research might help us?
How can we work together?
What might we try now?

Asking some of these questions at each grade level meeting or staff meeting over the course of a school year will have a tremendous impact on the school community and connections.

And what are our "takeaways" from writing this book? We are even more convinced about the importance of RI to children's overall development. We confirmed what we suspected—that many teachers are already paying attention to SEL and prioritizing RI in their classrooms, caring deeply about these issues, while also feeling pressured to focus on pacing and test prep. We will take away an enormous and growing respect for the profession of teaching and the teachers who are so open to learning in order to better serve their students. We have seen throughout this process that words like "love," "care," "trust," "connection," and "joy" are not distractions from learning; rather they are integral to the learning and lives of students, teachers, and schools who create a community together. This book has helped us to further appreciate the mutual benefits of research-practice partnerships and their potential to foster learning and growth for all involved. This book has brought us many insights and the deep motivation to continue the journey with our colleagues and friends. We hope our readers will join us as well.

Please visit the www.socionomy.net website to register and set up your surveys, and for more information and support.

References

Aboud, F. E., & Doyle, A. B. (1996). Parental and peer influences on children's racial attitudes. *International Journal of Intercultural Relations, 20*(3–4), 371–383.

Ahn, S., & Fedewa A. L. (2011). A meta-analysis of the relationship between children's physical activity and mental health. *Journal of Pediatric Psychology, 36*(4), 385–397.

Alvord, M., Uchino, B., & Wright, V. (2021). Manage stress: Strengthen your support network. American Psychological Association.

Bagwell, C. L., & Bukowski, W. M. (2018). *Friendship in childhood and adolescence: Features, effects, and processes.* In W. M. Bukowski, B. Laursen, & K. H. Rubin (Eds.), *Handbook of peer interactions, relationships, and groups* (2nd ed., pp. 371–390). The Guilford Press.

Barros, R. M., Silver, E. J., & Stein, R. E. K. (2009). School recess and group classroom behavior. *Pediatrics. 123*, 431–436.

Bento, G., & Dias, G. (2017). The importance of outdoor play for young children's healthy development. *Porto Biomedical Journal, 2*(5), 157–160. https://doi.org/10.1016/j.pbj.2017.03.003.

Berndt, T. J., & Keefe, K. (1995). Friends' influence on adolescents' adjustment to school. *Child Development, 66*(5), 1312–1329.

Boivin, M., Petitclerc, A., Feng, B., & Barker, E. D. (2010). The developmental trajectories of peer victimization in middle to late childhood and the changing nature of their behavioral correlates. *Merrill-Palmer Quarterly*, 231–260.

Borgatti, S. P., Everett, M. G., & Johnson, J. C. (2018). *Analyzing social networks.* Sage.

Brock, M. E., & Huber, H. B. (2017). Are peer support arrangements an evidence-based practice? A systematic review. *The Journal of Special Education, 51*(3), 150–163.

California Department of Education. (2023). Chronic Absenteeism Indicator FAQs. https://www.cde.ca.gov/ta/ac/cm/dbchronicfaq.asp#:~:text=A%20%22chronic%20absentee%22%20has%20been,taught%20in%20the%20regular%20day.

Carolan, B. V. (2013). *Social network analysis and education: Theory, methods & applications*. Sage Publications.

Carter, E. W., Asmus, J., Moss, C. K., Biggs, E. E., Bolt, D. M., Born, T. L., … & Weir, K. (2016). Randomized evaluation of peer support arrangements to support the inclusion of high school students with severe disabilities. *Exceptional Children, 82*(2), 209–233.

Centers for Disease Control and Prevention. (2011). Physical activity and health. http://www.cdc.gov/physicalactivity/everyone/health.

Coburn, C., & Penuel, W. R. (2016). Research-practice partnerships in education: Outcomes, dynamics and open questions. *Educational Researcher, 45*(1), 48 –54, DOI: 10.3102/0013189X16631750.

Cuadros, O., & Berger, C. (2016). The protective role of friendship quality on the wellbeing of adolescents victimized by peers. *Journal of Youth and Adolescence, 45*, 1877–1888.

DeLay, D., Zhang, L., Hanish, L. D., Miller, C. F., Fabes, R. A., Martin, C. L., … & Updegraff, K. A. (2016). Peer influence on academic performance: A social network analysis of social-emotional intervention effects. *Prevention Science, 17*, 903–913.

Delgado, M. Y., Ettekal, A. V., Simpkins, S. D., & Schaefer, D. R. (2016). How do my friends matter? Examining Latino adolescents' friendships, school belonging, and academic achievement. *Journal of Youth and Adolescence, 45*, 1110–1125.

Dyment, J. E., Bell, A. C., & Lucas, A. J. (2009). The relationship between school ground design and intensity of physical activity. *Child Geography, 7*(3), 261–276, DOI 10.1080/14733280903024423.

Erikson, E. H. (1968). *Identity youth and crisis* (No. 7). WW Norton & Company.

Erwin, H. E., Ickes, M., Ahn, S., & Fedewa, A. (2014). Impact of recess interventions on children's physical activity—A meta-analysis. *American Journal of Health Promotion, 28*, 159–167.

Estabrooks, P. A., Harden, S. M., Almeida, F. A., Hill, J. L., Johnson, S. B., Porter, G. C., Greenawald, M. H. (2019). Using integrated research-practice partnerships to move evidence-based principles into practice. *Exercises and Sports Sciences Review, 47*(3), 176–187. DOI: 10.1249/JES.0000000000000194.

Ferguson, S., Brass, N. R., Medina, M. A., & Ryan, A. M. (2022). The role of school friendship stability, instability, and network size in early adolescents' social adjustment. *Developmental Psychology, 58*(5), 950.

Gokhale, A. A. (2012). Collaborative learning and critical thinking. *Encyclopedia of the Sciences of Learning*, *88*, 634–636.

Handelzalts, A. (2009). *Collaborative curriculum development in teacher design teams*. Thesis (PhD). Twente University, The Netherlands.

Henrick, E. C., Cobb, P., Penuel, W. R., Jackson, K., & Clark, T. (2017). *Assessing Research-Practice Partnerships: Five Dimensions of Effectiveness*. New York, NY: William T. Grant Foundation.

Hirsh-Pasek, K., Golinkoff, R. M., Berk, L. E., & Singer, D. G. (2009). *A mandate for playful learning in school: Presenting the evidence*. New York, NY: Oxford University Press.

Holder, M. D., & Coleman, B. (2015). Children's friendships and positive well-being. In M. Demir (Ed.), *Friendship and happiness: Across the life-span and cultures* (pp. 81–97). Springer Science + Business Media.

Holt-Lunstad, J. (2022). Social connection as a public health issue: The evidence and a systemic framework for prioritizing the "social" in social determinants of health. *Annual Review of Public Health*, *43*, 193–213.

Huijboom F., Van Meeuwen P., Rusman E., & Vermeulen M. (2020) How to enhance teachers' professional learning by stimulating the development of professional learning communities: operationalising a comprehensive PLC concept for assessing its development in everyday educational practice. *Professional Development in Education*, *46*(5), 751–769, DOI: 10.1080/19415257.2019.1634630.

Jones, S. M., Barnes, S. P., Bailey, R., & Doolittle, E. J. (2017). Promoting social and emotional competencies in elementary school. *The Future of Children*, 49–72.

Kasari, C., Locke, J., Gulsrud, A., & Rotheram-Fuller, E. (2011). Social networks and friendships at school: Comparing children with and without ASD. *Journal of Autism and Developmental Disorders*, *41*(5), 533–544.

Kenneth R. Ginsburg, and the Committee on Communications, and the Committee on Psychosocial Aspects of Child and Family Health. (2007). The importance of play in promoting healthy child development and maintaining strong parent-child bonds. *Pediatrics*, *119*(1), 182–191. DOI:10.1542/peds.2006-2697.

Knifsend, C. A., Camacho-Thompson, D. E., Juvonen, J., & Graham, S. (2018). Friends in activities, school-related affect, and academic outcomes in diverse middle schools. *Journal of Youth and Adolescence*, *47*, 1208–1220.

Koster, M., Pijl, S. J., Nakken, H., & Van Houten, E. (2010). Social participation of students with special needs in regular primary education in the Netherlands. *International Journal of Disability, Development and Education*, *57*(1), 59–75.

Koster, M., Timmerman, M. E., Nakken, H., Pijl, S. J., & van Houten, E. J. (2009). Evaluating social participation of pupils with special needs in regular primary schools: Examination of a teacher questionnaire. *European Journal of Psychological Assessment*, *25*(4), 213.

Kurth, J. A., Lockman-Turner, E., Burke, K., & Ruppar, A. L. (2021). Curricular philosophies reflected in individualized education program goals for students with complex support needs. *Intellectual and Developmental Disabilities*, *59*(4), 283–294.

Ladd, G. W. (2017). Having friends, keeping friends, making friends, and being liked by peers in the classroom: Predictors of children's early school adjustment?. In *Interpersonal Development* (pp. 203–222). Routledge.

Lobstein, T., Baur, L., & Uauy, R. (2004). Obesity in children and young people: A crisis in public health. *Obesity Reviews*, *5*, pp. 4–85.

Mamas, C., & Trautman, D. (2023). Leading towards relational inclusivity for students identified as having special educational needs and disabilities. In Daly, A. J., & Liou, Y. H. (Eds.), *The relational leader: Catalyzing social networks for educational change*. Bloomsbury.

Mamas, C. (2013). Understanding inclusion in Cyprus. *European Journal of Special Needs Education*, *28*(4), 480–493.

Mamas, C., Daly, A. J., & Schaelli, G. H. (2019). Socially responsive classrooms for students with special educational needs and disabilities. *Learning, Culture and Social Interaction*, *23*, 100334.

Mamas, C., Daly, A. J., Struyve, C., Kaimi, I., & Michail, G. (2019). Learning, friendship and social contexts: Introducing a social network analysis toolkit for socially responsive classrooms. *International Journal of Educational Management*, *33*(6), 1255–1270.

Mamas. C., & Huang, D. (2022). Social network analysis software packages. In Frey B. (Ed.) *The SAGE encyclopedia of educational research, measurement, and evaluation (2nd* ed.*)*. Sage.

Mamas, C., Mejeh, M., & Michail, G. (in press). Understanding relational inclusivity through a social network analysis toolkit, *Handbook of Social Network Analysis and Education*.

Mamas, C., Schaelli, G. H., Daly, A. J., Navarro, H. R., & Trisokka, L. (2020). Employing social network analysis to examine the social participation of students identified as having special educational needs and disabilities. *International Journal of Disability, Development and Education, 67*(4), 393–408.

Mamas, C. & Trautman, D. (in press). Defining and exploring relational inclusivity through a social network analysis toolkit.

Maroulis, S., & Gomez, L. M. (2008). Does "connectedness" matter? Evidence from a social network analysis within a small-school reform. *Teachers College Record, 110*(9), 1901–1929.

McLeskey, J., Landers, E., Williamson, P., & Hoppey, D. (2012). Are we moving toward educating students with disabilities in less restrictive settings?. *The Journal of Special Education, 46*(3), 131–140.

O'Connor, E. A., Perdue, L. A., Coppola, E. L., Henninger, M. L., Thomas, R. G., & Gaynes, B. N. (2023). Depression and suicide risk screening: Updated evidence report and systematic review for the US Preventive Services Task Force. *JAMA, 329*(23), 2068–2085.

Ozbay, F., Johnson, D. C., Dimoulas, E., Morgan Iii, C. A., Charney, D., & Southwick, S. (2007). Social support and resilience to stress: From neurobiology to clinical practice. *Psychiatry (Edgmont), 4*(5), 35.

Pellegrini, A. D., Huberty, P. D., & Jones, I. (1995). The effects of recess timing on children's playground and classroom behaviors. *American Education Research Journal, 32*, 845–864.

Pratt, S. M., Imbody, S. M., Wolf, L. D., & Patterson, A. L. (2017). Co planning in co teaching: A practical solution. *Collaboration Forum, 52*, 243–249.

Qi, J., & Ha, A. S. (2012). Inclusion in physical education: A review of literature. *International Journal of Disability, Development and Education, 59*(3), 257–281.

Rogoff, B. (1990). *Apprenticeship in thinking: Cognitive development in social context.* Oxford University Press.

Rossetti, Z., & Keenan, J. (2018). The nature of friendship between students with and without severe disabilities. *Remedial and Special Education, 39*(4), 195–210.

Rotheram Fuller, E., Kasari, C., Chamberlain, B., & Locke, J. (2010). Social involvement of children with autism spectrum disorders in elementary school classrooms. *Journal of Child Psychology and Psychiatry, 51*(11), 1227–1234.

Ryabov, I. (2011). Adolescent academic outcomes in school context: Network effects reexamined. *Journal of Adolescence*, *34*(5), 915–927.

Schacter, H. L., Lessard, L. M., Kiperman, S., Bakth, F., Ehrhardt, A., & Uganski, J. (2021). Can friendships protect against the health consequences of peer victimization in adolescence? A systematic review. *School Mental Health*, 1–24.

Scheef, A., & Buyserie, B. (2020). Student development through involvement: Benefits of peer support arrangements. *Journal of At-Risk Issues*, *23*(2), 1–8.

Schwartz-Mette, R. A., Shankman, J., Dueweke, A. R., Borowski, S., & Rose, A. J. (2020). Relations of friendship experiences with depressive symptoms and loneliness in childhood and adolescence: A meta-analytic review. *Psychological Bulletin*, *146*(8), 664.

Slater, S. J., Nicholson, L., Chriqui, J., Turner, L., & Chaloupka, F., (2012). The impact of state laws and district policies on physical education and recess practices in a nationally representative sample of US public schools. *Archives of Pediatrics & Adolescent Medicine*, *166*(4), 311–316. doi:10.1001/archpediatrics.2011.1133.

Slavin, R. E. (2014). Cooperative learning and academic achievement: Why does groupwork work?.[Aprendizaje cooperativo y rendimiento académico:¿ por qué funciona el trabajo en grupo?]. *Anales de psicología/annals of psychology*, *30*(3), 785–791.

Slavin, R. E. (2015). Cooperative learning in elementary schools. *Education 3–13*, *43*(1), 5–14.

Smith, R. W., Barnes, I., Green, J., Reeves, G. K., Beral, V., & Floud, S. (2021). Social isolation and risk of heart disease and stroke: Analysis of two large UK prospective studies. *The Lancet Public Health*, *6*(4), e232–e239.

Tay, L., Tan, K., Diener, E., & Gonzalez, E. (2013). Social relations, health behaviors, and health outcomes: A survey and synthesis. *Applied Psychology: Health and Well-Being*, *5*(1), 28–78.

Tian, L., Chen, H., & Huebner, E. S. (2014). The longitudinal relationships between basic psychological needs satisfaction at school and school-related subjective well-being in adolescents. *Social Indicators Research*, *119*, 353–372.

Tucker, K., Sharp, G., Qingmin, S., Scinta, T., & Thanki, S. (2020). Fostering historically underserved students' success: An embedded peer support model that merges non-cognitive principles with proven academic support practices. *The Review of Higher Education*, *43*, 861–885.

Umberson, D., Crosnoe, R., & Reczek, C. (2010). Social relationships and health behavior across the life course. *Annual Review of Sociology*, *36*, 139–157.

van der Meulen, K., Granizo, L., & Del Barrio, C. (2021). Emotional peer support interventions for students with SEND: A systematic review. *Frontiers in Psychology*, *12*, 797913.

Van Mieghem, A., Verschueren, K., Petry, K., & Struyf, E. (2020). An analysis of research on inclusive education: A systematic search and meta review. *International Journal of Inclusive Education*, *24*(6), 675–689.

Vargas-Madriz, L. F., & Konishi, C. (2021). The relationship between social support and student academic involvement: The mediating role of school belonging. *Canadian Journal of School Psychology*, *36*(4), 290–303.

Vignery, K., & Laurier, W. (2020). Achievement in student peer networks: A study of the selection process, peer effects and student centrality. *International Journal of Educational Research*, *99*, 101499.

Vygotsky, L. S., & Cole, M. (1978). *Mind in society: Development of higher psychological processes*. Harvard University Press.

Yang, Y. C., Boen, C., Gerken, K., Li, T., Schorpp, K., & Harris, K. M. (2016). Social relationships and physiological determinants of longevity across the human life span. *Proceedings of the National Academy of Sciences*, *113*(3), 578–583.

Yu, X., Wang, X., Zheng, H., Zhen, X., Shao, M., Wang, H., & Zhou, X. (2023). Academic achievement is more closely associated with student-peer relationships than with student-parent relationships or student-teacher relationships. *Frontiers in Psychology*, *14*, 1012701.

Zeedyk, S. M., Cohen, S. R., Eisenhower, A., & Blacher, J. (2016). Perceived social competence and loneliness among young children with ASD: Child, parent and teacher reports. *Journal of Autism and Developmental Disorders*, *46*, 436–449.

Zeedyk, S. M., Rodriguez, G., Tipton, L. A., Baker, B. L., & Blacher, J. (2014). Bullying of youth with autism spectrum disorder, intellectual disability, or typical development: Victim and parent perspectives. *Research in Autism Spectrum Disorders*, *8*(9), 1173–1183.

Appendix

For Product Safety Concerns and Information please contact our
EU representative GPSR@taylorandfrancis.com Taylor & Francis
Verlag GmbH, Kaufingerstraße 24, 80331 München, Germany